THE THEOLOGY OF PRAISE

THE
THEOLOGY
OF
PRAISE

Jan Milic Lochman

JOHN KNOX PRESS
ATLANTA

Scripture quotations in this publication are from the King James Version of the Bible.

Library of Congress Cataloging in Publication Data

Lochman, Jan Milic.
   The theology of praise.

   1. Lord's prayer. 2. Christian life–Reformed
authors. 3. Christianity–20th century. 4. Praise
of God. I. Title.
BV231.8.L62   231   81–82370
ISBN 0-8042-0730-5 (pbk.) AACR2

10 9 8 7 6 5 4 3 2 1
Printed in the United States of America
John Knox Press
Atlanta, Georgia 30365

CONTENTS

INTRODUCTION

There are not many words used as frequently and regularly in the common worship and private devotions of Christian people as the sentence, *"For thine is the kingdom and the power and the glory, for ever. Amen."* This is the best known Christian doxology, the concluding confession of the Lord's Prayer. This very fact, however, indicates not only the frequency but also the theological significance of the text. "Doxology" means praise, adoration, and glorification of God. Taken from the theological viewpoint, "the chief end of human life is to glorify God." If this is true, as the catechisms of our churches, particularly those of the Reformed tradition, again and again emphasize, then doxology is not only the matter of solemn liturgical proclamation but the very constitution of a truly Christian (and truly human) existence.

In his "Institutes," John Calvin elaborates this fundamental importance of our doxology: "This is firm and tranquil repose for our faith. For if our prayers were to be commended to God by our worth, who would dare even mutter in his presence? Now, however miserable we may be, though unworthiest of all, however devoid of all commendation, we will yet never lack a reason to pray, never be shorn of assurance, since his Kingdom, power and glory can never be snatched away from our Father" (*Institutes* III, 20, 47).

The pages that follow do not present an overall balanced exposition of our sentence. They rather take up the three central motives in it and relate them to some of the most burning issues of our contemporary world. I am well aware of the danger of subjective selectivity involved in such an approach. But the risky approach might lead us closer to the original "Sitz im Leben" of this old Christian doxology. Its words do not appear in the oldest manuscripts of the Lord's Prayer. Evidently, they were added to it by the early church. "This is the praise of the becoming church ready to start its difficult earthy pilgrimage" (E. Lohmeyer, *Das Vater-unser,* p. 174). Are we not in a similar situation today? In many countries, our churches face rather difficult trials. I think of my own experiences out of the pressures upon and within Christian congregations in a Marxist society in Czechoslovakia. But I think also of the spiritual challenges confronting a Christian mission in a secularized, affluent country such as Switzerland. And I do not forget the confessing struggle of Christians in the countries of the "Third World" like Korea. In all the "three worlds" our ecumenical pilgrimage is full of difficulties and challenges.

Nevertheless, we Christian people do not stop praying "thine is the kingdom and the power and the glory for ever." What exactly do we do in such a prayer? A Christian prayer is not a magical operation that would stand in itself in a sort of "splendid isolation" aloof from the concrete circumstances in which we pray and live. The older Karl Barth used to say: "To clasp the hands in prayer is the beginning of an uprising against the disorder of the world."

Here, the questions could and should be asked: In what way does the classical doxology of our faith illuminate the concrete conditions of our life? What horizon is opened by it for us to see more and to move forward? In what direction do the three central motives "kingdom," "power," "glory" orient and motivate our personal and social pilgrimage?

In three attempts I would like to address myself to such questions.

I

THINE
IS THE
KINGDOM

The Impact of the Kingdom of God

What are the issues at stake where the biblical message of the *kingdom of God* is concerned? Here we need a look at the New Testament. "The kingdom of God is at hand; repent, and believe the gospel!"—this, according to Mark 1:15, is the first word of Jesus of Nazareth, the fundamental principle and cardinal point of his ministry right from the start. All that follows in the rest of the evangelist's narrative is in a certain sense a commentary on this fundamental principle. The message of Jesus is the good news of the coming kingdom of God, of its liberating promise and claim. Think only of the parables of Jesus: almost all of them turn upon the mystery of the kingdom. Or think, above all, of the Sermon on the Mount. What have we here if not the constitutive articles and the guidelines of the kingdom? Still more important, it is not only in the words of Jesus Christ but also in his deeds that the kingdom of God is represented, not merely in theory but also in practice. For example, we read in his healings: "If I by the finger of God cast out demons, no doubt the kingdom of God is come upon you" (Luke 11:20). Further, and in a still more profound way, we read that his sufferings—supremely in his cross and resurrection— are the reign of God in action. This is the view we find in the whole New Testament: throughout the path taken by the man of Nazareth, from the cradle to the cross and to the empty tomb, the kingdom of God is upon us.

The consequences? "Repent, and believe!"—that is to say, hearts and circumstances are to be changed. They are to be changed in the disciples' circle first. Then the consequences are to reach through them "into all the world," and emerge in the Christian mission with truly world-transforming results. The human world is set in motion. But—let there be no misunderstandings!—the change will come not from private initiative but in discipleship. To put it differently, it will not come in voluntaristic or activistic ardor and impetuosity but in the power—in the breakthrough—of the kingdom. But again: this power is here; the work has become different in the course of the history of Jesus Christ; hence it can and must become different also in Christian discipleship. *Status mundi renovabitur* ("the state of the world will be renewed")—as the Hussites pregnantly summed up their revolutionary view of faith and the world in the light of the coming kingdom of God. The "revolution of the kingdom of God"—I know that such a phrase sounds almost bombastic and that it is also open to misunderstanding. Yet given a biblical content, it meets the case. That at least is how the consequences of the kingdom have been understood and lived out in the course of history by loyal witnesses of the kingdom of God—and I mean this in a comprehensive, certainly not sectarian, sense.

Karl Barth in his early days once took up the question of the relationship between the kingdom of God and everyday life and, with his eye upon the Bad Boll of the Blumhardts, characterized this relationship as follows:

The new, New Testament element that emerged again in Bad Boll can be summed up in the one word, hope—hope of a visible and tangible *manifestation* of God's sovereignty over the world (in contrast to the mere—often so blasphemous—talk of the omnipotence of God)—hope of radical *help* and radical rescue from the world of yesterday (in contrast to all those soothing and consoling promises that must everywhere evaporate in face of the inevitable order of things)—hope for all, for *mankind* (in contrast to the selfish concern for the salvation of one's own soul and in contrast to all attempts to breed aristocratic religious supermen)—hope for the *corporal side* of life as well as for the spiritual side, in the sense that not only sin and sorrow, but also poverty, sickness and death will one day be done away (in contrast to the purely spiritual ideal of so-called "ethico-religious" life). ("Vergangenheit and Zukunft" in *Anfange der dialektischen Theologie* I, ed. Moltmann, p. 45).

It is the reality of this hope in all its many strafications that is at stake in our repentance and in our faith, in our "seeking after the kingdom of God," in our "Christian existence."

The Power of Structural Constraints

Yet at this point many of us begin to have doubts and scruples: does such a view not flatly ask too much of us as Christians and as a church in our situation today? The promises of the kingdom of God are all very well, but the practical circumstances—they are a different story. To put it concretely and bluntly: what can the message of the kingdom of God achieve in face of the *structural constraints of the day?* This brings us to the second part of our heading. It represents an attempt to address hard facts which for many of our contemporaries bar any prospect of the kingdom of God and make it look as though its relationship to reality were an illusion. These facts cannot be avoided. That is to say, they have to be faced both in theology and the church if we do not intend to bypass the challenges and needs of the day.

What does it mean to speak of structural constraints? Very often the term refers simply, and vaguely, to a dubious aspect of contemporary society—namely, the tendency in modern economics and politics to get people in hand wherever possible. I say "contemporary society" because this tendency is present in different forms in different systems. In the background of my own experience it is particularly striking in East European "realized socialist" society with its permanent attempt to bring every important area of people's lives under control from a single ideological and political center. But a similar tendency can be perceived in the Western capitalistic world, albeit in a more finely differentiated and more pluralistic form. These are the structural constraints of a competitive market economy which in its own way also tends to regard people as consumers or dependent workers and then by gentle enticement or perceptible economic pressure to "condition" them to the conduct that is considered desirable.

We must beware of simplifying. We have to avoid an easily suggested misunderstanding, a theological short-circuit which appears at this point. This is, the temptation to pass a wholly negative, if not indeed "demonizing," judgment on structural constraints. A temptation of this kind is particularly strong in the circles in which Protestant theology is oriented towards existentialism or pietism. It is, however, not without foundation. The tendencies in question do indeed have their strange, and estranging, aspects. These include the subjection to the anonymous powers of the "done thing" against which the existentialists warn us and the underestimation of the personal decision before God which is so important to the pietists. Such things are indeed dangerous to an authentically human and Christian existence. Yet we are heading for a theological and ethical short-circuit if this concern for the inner authenticity of personal human existence is extended till it becomes a vote of no confidence towards the external world. That is to say, if realms of our material and social activity in economics and politics are underestimated or even dismissed as being ultimately only "unauthentic" *(Uneigentliches)*. Such an attitude is theologically dubious because it suggests a division between our inner and outer world—a division which from the standpoint of the biblical (as distinct from the idealistic) understanding of humanity cannot be maintained in this form: people in the Bible are all of a piece, and also social beings, the "souls of their bodies," the fellows of their fellowcreatures. And it is ethically problematical because (by underestimating the outward conditions of personal decision) it makes human responsibility a private matter—and morally asks too much of us. Here the Marxist correction—not Marxist dogma—must be accepted in self-critical terms: "The essence of man is not something abstract that dwells in the single individual. In reality it is the ensemble of social circumstances" (Karl Marx, "Die sechste These über Feuerbach," in *Die Fruhschriften,* ed. S. Landshut, p. 340). People are (certainly not exclusively, but also) the *"world of people."*

Perhaps the German word *Sachzwang* can help us to a subtler differentiation. I am no great friend of this term—not only because I can hardly translate it into my own language but above all because it can so easily be misused: premature talk of *"Sachzwang"* often veils the fact that "tangible material interests" are at stake. " 'Things' are less constraining than they are pretended to be; but it is true that *our* interest in profit and power determines what is done with 'things' and how processes take place" (D. Schellong, "Illusion Ethik," in *Reformatio 26th Year,* 1977, p. 555). Critical examination of explicitly asserted "structural constraints"—e.g., the model argument often thought to be conclusive: "Whoever says A must also say B" (e.g., "Whoever wants to save unemployment must build atomic power stations")—is always necessary in this field. Yet with this proviso the German term with its bipartite form could help us to discern, and to bear in mind, the problems thereby designated: *Sach-Zwang* ("thing—constraint"). Constraint

(Zwang) in every form—ecclesiastical, ideological, technocratical—must be opposed. On the other hand objectivity— (Sachlichkeit—bearing in mind the concrete state of things or *Sachverhalte*—the objective conditions, circumstances, and structures in which we are involved along with other people in each specific case—is desirable.

It is not easy to distinguish the two aspects of the structural constraints. As in the oneness of the German word *Sach-Zwang,* so they are bound up together in the oneness of reality. This gives rise to tensions that can mislead us into short-circuit alternatives. One mistaken alternative is a retreat into the inward realms of existence, a renunciation of the world of objects. Another is a flight into the thicket of circumstances and systems in which the "subjugation mechanisms" are so heavily stressed that any form of personal ethics seems an illusion. Both attitudes really amount to a moral capitulation in face of structural constraints that have become a fetish—an approach, which seems to me hardly justifiable from the standpoint of the Bible. To my mind a "Christian existence amid the structural constraints of the day" would have to seek a more finely differentiated orientation and adopt some other way.

How are we to define this other way more precisely? What is it in terms of content? Such questions bring us to the heart of our subject. We shall now attempt to take its two poles as we have just described them—the "kingdom of God" and the "structural constraints of the day"—and bring them into a mutual relationship that will certainly be full of tension. It should, however, also be a meaningful relationship. While this is a difficult task, it has to be done if Christians are not to give up being Christians. There are three lines which I should now like to address. While these three will admittedly not be a final completion of the task, they will certainly be an attempt to clarify the perspectives on our common path.

Overcoming the Spirit of Fatalism

We recall that the kingdom of God as proclaimed by Jesus and present in him breaks in upon the world and sets it moving. The spell of old customs, of the eternal has-beens, is broken. One could also say that the kingdom of God bursts history open, sets it in motion—in a direction that is quite specific— *viz.,* towards our liberation in all the many stratifications in which we are endangered and enslaved.

I have already quoted a word of Jesus that is at first perhaps startling but ultimately liberating: "If I by the finger of God cast out demons, no doubt the kingdom of God is come upon you." One could also put it the other way round: if the kingdom of God is come upon us, no doubt demons will be cast out—the old ones and the new, in the literal and in the figurative sense. This effect of what happens in the kingdom of God has been sketched by H.J. Iwand as follows: "It means that to an inconceivable extent the world is disenchanted and man liberated. It is inevitable, where this happens, that the bolts should be drawn and the bars broken by which men are enslaved to those principalities and powers that have their roots in death and the law. It must be the day of liberation that here dawns" (*Nachgelassene Werke,* vol. 2, p. 14).

In the advent of Jesus Christ—and, incomparably, on Easter morning—such a day of liberation has in fact dawned. The human world has been de-fatalized. This was the liberating impact of faith in the kingdom of God—already in the New Testament, and then in the missionary activity it gave rise to in the early church. Most people in the hellenistic age lived under the shadow of fatalistic constraints, surrendered to the superior might of ominous "principalities and powers." The apostles related the message of the kingdom of God to these fatalities. They did not mean to dispute their existence or the dangers they might cause human life. Yet they recognized that in the long run these forces are no match for the power of the kingdom of God. Jesus Christ has proved himself the master of all powers. Hence in him the power of fate is broken. In view of him we are accordingly no longer slaves but the "free people of the creation." Our world is not a reality dominated by fate and unalterably sealed. The renewing of hearts and circumstances is a possibility in the perspective of the kingdom of God; repentance and faith are needed.

I do not maintain that this "apostolic lesson" can be taken over and applied "without a hitch" to our existence amid the structural constraints of the day. The structural constraints of our day are not by any means to be equated with the fatalities of the hellenistic world-view. Yet there are also astonishing parallels. Do our "structural constraints" not all too often also show signs of the tendency to fatalism? Does the weight, both in theory and reality, not all too often shift from the structure to the constraint? Is the very necessary reference to structural components in social and economic processes not all too often manipulated into would-be necessities? Today, both the tendency to fatalism and fetishism has to be resisted. Here it is a help to remember that the Christian hope of the kingdom is fundamentally the resistance movement against fatalism. In confrontation with the structural constraints and amid the feelings of impotence and rage by which they are often accompanied, we must initiate this hope and testify to it.

Christians should at all events not be the first to capitulate fatalistically before the charms or the pressures of "structural constraints." Repentance and faith—and not blind persistence in "going on"—are the "virtues of the kingdom." A Christian existence amid the structural constraints of the day should express both repentance and faith and find buoyancy in them. We must be guided by both in our personal style of living. We should also seek both virtues in a readiness to analyze in sober terms the complex designated by the concept "structural constraint," and in finding our social response on new "paths amid the danger" (C. F. von Weizsacker).

Promises and Circumstances

In my second approach to the attempt to define the meaning of the kingdom of God for Christian existence amid the structural constraints of our day, I should like to put forward the caption *"Promises and Circumstances."* In so doing I am thinking of a biblical text which in recent years has played a special role in ecumenical discussions, of the "Nazareth Manifesto" (as it has occasionally been called)—*viz.,* Luke 4:18-22, the "first sermon of Jesus." The text has already an important bearing on our topic for the simple reason that it is the Lucan parallel to Mark's summary statement on the first appearance of Jesus. The heart of the passage is: "The Spirit of the Lord is upon me, because he hath anointed me; he hath sent me to preach good tidings to the poor, to preach deliverance to the captives and recovering of sight to the blind, to liberate them that are bruised and let them go free, to preach the acceptable year of the Lord."

This is a quotation from Isaiah, the fundamental statement of the hope of Israel, the promise of the coming, liberating, and reconciling future of God. The whole sermon of Jesus on this text is reproduced in the brief phrase: "Today is this scripture fulfilled in your ears." A short sermon, yet it serves to mark Jesus' "program of the kingdom of God." What Isaiah had promised for the final, messianic future of God, Jesus declares to be valid for the present. The hope of liberation and reconciliation is for him no song of the distant future, a uptopian dream out of touch with reality. The promises are bursting in upon our circumstances and conditions.

This is to pave the way for a *new understanding of reality.* No fanatical or enthusiastic view: the circumstances are taken seriously. It is in fact particularly striking how sharply the speaker's eye is focused on the manifold conditions and dangers in the human world. For Isaiah and Jesus there is no fleeing to the heights of heaven. On the contrary, they plumb the depths of the highly realistic circumstances that oppress us all. The people of suffering, as groups and as individuals, are named in concrete and obligatory terms. They see the poor—those who have had too much of the short end in life in economic terms, the hungry and the unemployed. And they recognize the poor in the moral or even religious sense, those who have been underestimated, overlooked, shunned by the official church and by society, those eyed with suspicion in the church. They name the captives—fellow human beings who belong to the oppressed or the fallen and are at the mercy, or rather mercilessness, of their rulers, the bondservants and slaves who have been robbed of their freedom and their human rights in the name of law and order. The blind, too—the hampered in body and soul, the sick, whose possibilities in life have been foreshortened. And the bruised—people who have been shipwrecked by buffetings from without or failure and collapse from within. They are all there, the whole human race, each of us with his own particular need. There is no doubt about it: Jesus (and that means the kingdom of God) does not bypass the circumstances and oppressing constraints of his day. On the contrary, he states them by name: poverty, loss of freedom, sickness, bruisedness.

Yet this undisguised picture of things is, in the light of the message of the kingdom of God, not the *whole* of reality. The whole human race, each of us with his own particular concrete need, but not isolated, not left on his own, not surrendered to the naked force of circumstances, but set within the power circuit of the coming kingdom of God, in the perspective of promise. This at all events is how Jesus puts it, speaking in the train of the Prophets. To the poor—glad tidings; to the captives —liberation; to the blind—recovery of sight; to the bruised— salvation. Comprehensive and variously stratified is our human need. But also comprehensive and variously stratified is the promise of God. Blumhardt and Barth, as we recall from the quotation cited above, were right in their understanding and exposition of the hope of the kingdom in its many-sided relationship to reality.

This, then, is the way faith in the kingdom of God understands reality and links up with reality. Circumstances—and these, too, in the earthliest possible terms, in terms of corporeality, economics, historical, material things. But *not* on their own, isolated, turned into an unchangeable, inviolable fundamental principle of reality, i.e., no biologism, no economism, and no historical materialism. For the world of people, the reality in which we live means not only circumstances but also the promises that bear upon them, the world in the light of the coming kingdom of God—a reality which cannot be grasped by any computer, but which, if we take Jesus' word for it, is nevertheless here, appealing to us and, above all, liberating us and setting us in motion.

This open understanding of, and relationship to, reality has to find representation in our Christian existence amid the structural constraints of the day. The structures have to be taken seriously, otherwise religion becomes the opiate of the people. The constraints must not be allowed to gain the day, otherwise we Christians become salt without savor. Above all we have to find Christian ways of counteracting every suggestion of, and every pincer movement by, any kind of "one-dimensional" explanation and administration of human affairs. Human beings are not merely the "world of people"; their essence is more than an "ensemble of social circumstances." We humans are heirs of the promise. We cannot be reckoned up in terms of one dimension.

It is in persistent reference to this fact that I see the abiding and, in view of the ever-growing structural constraints, increasingly relevant contribution of the church in the midst of modern society, in East and West. This at least is my own experience as I have lived through it, with refreshing clarity above all in the East. I have learned that it makes an essential difference to the cultural and social climate of society whether there are groups of Christian people in its midst who, perhaps sorely tried, yet not misled by the structural constraints of the day, keep open the prospect of the kingdom of God, not only for themselves and the church, but also for their society. When the circumstances are confronted by promises, this helps to awaken, and to keep awake, the unresting search that is so necessary to us all—the search for a *"plus ultra,"* for more humane space, human solidarity amid the structural constraints of the day.

Righteousness and Joy

So far we have spoken in rather general terms of tendencies, structures, constraints in our living conditions today. We can and should, however, be specific—even when we are aware of the fact that a concrete example is possible only in the everyday lives of our churches. In preparing this material I had at my disposal the evaluation of an inquiry carried out by the Reformed Church in the German Federal Republic on the subject of "structural constraints," and I should like to take this as my starting point. Here two constraints obviously stand in the forefront: the constraint in our society to consume, and the constraint to achieve. Without consumption and achievement, there are "no flourishing economy, no investments, perhaps not even the possibility of giving development aid." The report goes on to say, "I am compelled to live in a social order whose wellbeing, in which I have part, largely depends on the fact that other peoples—in fact half the world—are economically exploited."

There is no denying that these remarks do in fact envisage burning problems of our social Here and Now. There are many among us, especially in the younger generation, who would associate them with the Western economic and political system —that is to say, they would interpret the structural constraints of our society as being the subjugation mechanisms of capitalism. I should be more cautious here; for indeed I cannot forget that these constraints, above all the constraint to achieve, are also very much at home in "realized socialism." In addition, the order of democratic society includes other motives and forces that run athwart the capitalistic element in our system and do not capitulate before it. Yet the fact does remain that this capitalistic element in our system, the one-sided direction of personal and communal life towards profit, growth and achievement, is highly problematical. It cannot be passed over in silence, especially in discussing the structural constraints of our day in the light of the kingdom of God.

For the kingdom of God quite plainly puts forward priorities that are other than the unbridled urge to possess. "Seek ye first the kingdom of God!"—this word of Jesus defines the true priority in Christian existence. It is, of course, not left hanging in the air, but it stands in the concrete context of a decisive renunciation of the life of care, of self-obsession, of avidity. The fundamental values and modes of behavior that are set up as priorities by the kingdom of God are different from all this, and indeed run counter to it. Think only of the Beatitudes, of the whole Sermon on the Mount, and of the first sermon of Jesus in Nazareth, that we have already stressed. We see here the matter of being rather than having—and this, too, the *new* being in a co-humanity that stands under the grace of God and faces towards our neighbor. It is from this standpoint—and accordingly athwart and against the tendencies designated by the expressions "constraint to consume" and "constraint to achieve"—that the disciples of Jesus have to come to grips with the structural constraints of the day.

There are *two priorities,* two "marks" of the kingdom of

God, that I would mention as points of orientation—righteous-ness and joy. "Seek ye first the kingdom of God—and his *righteousness!*" What is laid down by the Bible as the goal of a meaningful human life is never merely private happiness and salvation, but righteousness before God and before our neigh-bors—justification and justice. That is how Paul interprets the history and destiny of Jesus. And that is how the history of God with his people is understood already in the Old Testament: the covenant of God is the covenant of peace and justice. The concept of the kingdom of God gives clear expression to the very fact that this is the outlook of the Bible story—God and his kingdom, his kingdom and his righteousness, cannot be separated. "For the kingdom of God is not eating and drinking (so to speak circling around, and fighting over, the attractions of consuming), but righteousness" (Rom. 14:17).

It is no accident that the message of the kingdom of God, where it has been effective in history, has found a hearing and a following more particularly among Christians who are so-cially awake and involved. Today, too, it urges righteousness and right upon us—which, in Jesus' sense, means taking the part of the poor and of those who have been robbed of their rights—here and now, beyond our doors, in our city, but also out beyond the walls of our city, beyond the frontiers of our land, in the world that is so drastically marked and endangered by circumstances of unrighteousness. For us this means that if we plot our course in life by values other than those of the "Sun of Righteousness," then the kingdom of God will become a judgment upon us. A Christian existence that fails at this point and gives way to such alien constraints as possession and con-sumption becomes salt without savor.

The first word of the kingdom of God is justice, but the last word—inseparably bound up with the first—is *joy.* I have just quoted a word of the Apostle's on the state of the kingdom of God—but I did not quote it all. It goes on to add something

that cannot be ignored: "The kingdom of God is . . . righteousness and peace and *joy in the Holy Spirit.*" The fact is that with
this addition Paul takes up an element that is fundamentally
constitutive in Jesus' message of the kingdom of God. It is
surely striking how often, for example in the parables, the note
of joy is struck. The kingdom of God appears indeed to be the
"sum total of joy: the marriage, the feast, the harvest. The
Gospel gives rise to astounded joy. The happiness of the new
beginning would have itself put on record. There is feasting,
jubilation, and dancing" (H. J. Kraus, *Reich, Gottes-Reich der
Freiheit,* p. 22). The different atmosphere is this: repentance
and faith in the kingdom—seeking his righteousness—do not
have the nature of a "must" or a constraint. They are a "may"
and a liberation. H. J. Kraus rightly says: "The coming of the
kingdom of God means the issuing of the universal amnesty of
forgiveness. A totally new, incomparable beginning is made. If
we overlook or bypass this event, determining all else as it does,
then we shall never realize what the kingdom of God is. We
shall be surrendering this kingdom to human interest and
human utopias, even if we do so with the most determined
theocratic intentions" (op. cit.).

A Christian existence amid the structural constraints of
the day will surely not allow this atmosphere of joy to be left
out. It will especially avoid the constraint to achieve, which
dominates and destroys so much in our lives, including our
church lives. Nothing against labor in the sense of work! But
everything against achievement in the sense of justification by
works, as an attempt to justify systems and individuals! The
convulsive effort to justify ourselves and be justified by our
works, the constraint of having to legitimate ourselves, is perhaps in both the East and the West *the* temptation of our day.
If achievement is taken merely as an instrument for the concrete maintaining and developing of life it is one thing. If,
however, it is regarded as the ultimate factor that gives life a

meaning; if human relationships are calculated above all according to their potential value in terms of profit and consumption; if the morals of society are one-sidedly measured in terms of the "productive" and the "successful"; if children and old folk (the privileged in the kingdom of God), the short-comers and the shipwrecked are openly or covertly felt to be a burden and treated as such—then the "merciless consequences" of justification by works and of the constraint of self-legitimation will soon be crushingly felt.

The kingdom of God, however, is the offer of grace and the assault of Jesus upon the "gracelessness" of hearts and circumstances. It is the triumph of grace—and hence a gushing spring of joy—in the midst of creation. There is no more meaningful task for a Christian existence amid the structural constraints of the day than to see to it that in the praise of God and the persistent advocacy of grace—despite all the evil spirits of the day—this gushing spring of righteousness, peace, and joy in the Holy Spirit is not allowed to run dry. "For thine is the kingdom, and the power, and the glory."

II
THINE
IS THE
POWER

The Power of Grace and the Graceless Powers

Contradictory Prophecy

A little less than a hundred years ago two of the most influential thinkers of the day expressed themselves in particularly pointed terms on the *question of power*. They did so at the University of Basel where they looked back upon the same phenomena of world history and forward to the coming twentieth century. But they came to opposite conclusions and evaluations. *Friedrich Nietzsche* uttered an indignant and conclusive repudiation of the traditional Christian and democratic "herd morality" with its ideals of "equality of rights," "sympathy for all suffering things," and "security and peace." This leads, he said, to a general flatness and decadence of the human race. The "future lords of the earth" must adopt other ways. The elevation of the human type requires "hardness, violence, and danger both on our streets and in our hearts. Inequality of rights are necessary." Our future, he maintains, lies in the intensified will to live, "even to the extent of an unconditional will to power and to supremacy" (F. Nietzsche, *Werke,* III, p. 468).

How different is Nietzsche's colleague and friend, the historian *Jacob Burckhardt!* The outcome of his "Reflexions on

World History" and the upshot of his message to the coming
century is an emphatic warning: When the course of European
political history is subjected to sober examination, he maintains, there emerges—above all in view of its absolutist tendencies on the right and the left (Burckhardt is here thinking of
"Louis XIV, of Napoleon and of the revolutionary Peoples'
Republics")—a sinister urge to power. "And power is evil in
itself, no matter who exercises it. Power is not a permanent
reality. It is, rather, a lust, and for that very reason insatiable.
Hence it is in itself unhappy and must accordingly lead to
unhappy results. . . . Historic greatness takes it for granted that
its primary task is to assert and increase itself, and power does
not better man one whit" (*Weltgeschichtliche Betrachtungen*, p.
131).

When we consider the developments in the world history
of our century, then we can hardly evade the conclusion that
the contradictory prophecy of the two Baselers in their expectations and fears has been largely confirmed. Our century bears
the ominous mark of unprecedentedly intensified and menacing
power. This power has exploded in particularly spectacular
ways in the most cruel wars history has hitherto known. Today
it lurks behind the extremely unstable "balance of dread," with
its store of weapons whose destructive power is capable of
putting an end to our life on this planet. In terms of the political
state it has found particularly sharp crystallization in the cynical power systems of Nazi or Stalinist totalitarianism and has
become a temptation also in other forms of state. Even in the
Western democracies, in view of certain authoritarian tendencies, we could rightly speak of the "arrogance of power" (J.W.
Fulbright). In economic terms it has been at work in the structures of national and international exploitation, the victims of
which have been the economically weak classes and peoples.
And technological power, in the last century still celebrated as
the force of unequivocal progress, has in our century soon also

shown its "other side," as a potential source of technocratical alienation and ecological danger.

To be sure, we must not oversimplify. The developments we have just mentioned have not all simply been allowed free course. Everywhere counterforces have been aroused and mobilized—for example, in the realm of ecumenical Christianity. This, too, belongs to the history of our century. Yet on the whole Nietzsche and Burckhardt—in the concord of their dissonance—are admittedly right: the question of power has become the fundamental problem of our life and survival. We live in a world of "grace-less powers."

In this power-laden and indeed power-possessed world the Christian church confesses and prays day by day its doxology: "For thine is the kingdom and *the power* and the glory, for ever and ever. Amen." What happens when in the world of powers we recall and appeal to the power and might of God? Does this mean that more or less in Nietzsche's sense the human will to power is, after all, rendered legitimate? Or does it perhaps rather mean, in Burckhardt's sense, the start of a Christian protest song? Or—does nothing happen at all as far as earthly relationships are concerned? Are the words of the doxology used as a solemn pointer towards pious regions that have nothing whatever to do with the question of worldly power? All these possibilities have been considered and tried out in the course of church history. I think the problems concerned are among the most pressing challenges to ecumenical theology and social ethics.

The Power of God

The experience of power is normally a rudimentary part of religion. This is demonstrated unequivocally by the general study of the phenomenology of religion. "Mana," "orenda," "vakanda" are fundamental concepts of the history of religion: they all express experiences of power. The superiority of the

forces of nature, the menace of superior animals, the extraordinary capacities of holy or powerful people, or even overwhelm-
ing aesthetic impressions—all these are experienced as forces
and powers. The human's reaction since primeval times has
been one of wonder, amazement, reverence, and often even of
fear. This encourages religious modes of conduct, cultic or
magical practices.

When the figures and ideas of gods arise in the course of
the history of religion, statements of power are applied to them
almost as a matter of course: the powerful is understood ultimately as divine, the divine primarily as powerful. And when
the thought of the one and only God is conceived, the corresponding predication of power is also intensified: the one God
is confessed not only to be powerful, but to be all-powerful. This
has its transparent logic: "How could being be attributed to
God in any other way than as powerful being, and thus the
all-powerful being of a King of all kings and Lord of all lords?"
(G. Ebeling, *Dogmatik* III, p. 478). The Bible, too, is surely rich
in expressions that are used to confess and to praise the power,
might, and glory of God. The doxology of the Lord's Prayer is
an example of this. And as for the church's dogmatic efforts,
it can be noted that the Christian creed, too, employs in its first
sentence as the sole predicate of God the Father the unequivocal term, almighty. The power of God is conceived as omnipotence.

Yet it would be misleading if the biblical statement, "thine
is the power," were to be understood in terms of the general
manistic thought of power or the general theistic thought of
omnipotence. Examinations of the biblical expressions for
power and might that are undertaken from the standpoint of
philology and of the history of theology (as, for example, in
Kittel's *Theol. Worterbuch*) point out essential differences. It is
a typical mark of the ideas of "mana" and "orenda" that they
are considered impersonal. They are thought of primarily in the

context of nature: it is a case of magically given, irresistibly dominating power that leaves no room for argument. It is consistent with this that sorcery and magic are the reactions and methods here preferred.

The biblical conceptions of the power and might of God only marginally display manistic features (for example, in Old Testament stories of the ark of the covenant in 1 Samuel). In the mainstream of the biblical testimony the witness to the power of God is essentially different, namely, *personal and related to history*. "The place of the neutral idea of god is taken by the personal God. The place of the neutral forces of nature is taken by the power and might of the personal God" (W. Grundmann, in *Theol. Worterbuch zum NT* II, p. 292). And: "The power of God has according to his will and purpose a character that is formative of history and constitutive of history" (*op. cit.,* p. 293). For this reason personal prayer and historical involvement—not sorcery and magic—are the responses in keeping with the power of God.

This idea in the biblical thought of power becomes clear when we consider the contexts in which the concept receives its biblical stamp. In the *Old Testament* we have to take account above all of the *event of the exodus,* the departure of Israel from Egypt and its rescue at the Red Sea. This event stands without doubt in the center of the Israelite faith. Apart from it there would surely be no Yahweh religion, and there would be no covenant people Israel. It is precisely from this event of the exodus and the covenant that the essential Old Testament definitions of the power of God arise. This happens right from the start, in the immediate course of the exodus, in Israel's song of thanksgiving and praise: "Thy right hand, O Lord, is majestic in strength. . . . In thy constant love thou hast led the people whom thou didst ransom: thou hast guided them by thy strength to thy holy dwellingplace" (Exod. 15:6,13). And in prophetic reminiscence the power of God is praised no less emphatically in view of the same liberating event: "O Lord God, thou hast made the heavens and the earth by thy great strength and with thy outstretched arm; nothing is impossible for thee. . . . Thou didst bring thy people Israel out of Egypt with signs and portents, with a strong hand and an outstretched arm, and with terrible power" (Jer. 32:17,21). The God who has done this, who has given a liberating start to the history of his people in face of the superiority of their oppressors, and who thereafter through hundreds and thousands of years has ever and again proved himself in hours of personal and historical oppression to be the faithful covenant God—this is "the great and mighty God whose name is the Lord of hosts, great are thy purposes and mighty thy actions" (Jer. 32:18).

The relation to the exodus and the event of the covenant have to be kept in view if we would do justice to the Old Testament thought of the power and might of God. Let us not forget this: its specific characteristics are accordingly liberation and faithfulness to the covenant.

A similar situation is to be found in the New Testament. Just as the Old Testament testimony to the power of God is anchored in the event of the exodus, so the *New Testament* testimony to his power is anchored in the *event of Christ.* The life story and and the lifestyle of Jesus are already important here. In the testimony of the evangelists and in the recollection of the apostles, Jesus of Nazareth is portrayed as the true bearer of power. His power can even be "palpably" felt in his extraordinary acts. In the New Testament they are repeatedly described as *"dynameis,"* "acts of power" (cf. Matt. 11: 20f.; 13: 58; Mark 6: 2; Luke 19: 37; Acts 2: 22 etc.). However, the magical and miraculous elements here appear to be marginal in the ideas and expectations of the people. Think, for example, of the story of the healing of the woman with the issue of blood (Mark 5: 25f.). From the standpoint of the evangelists and of Jesus himself his wonders are no magical miracles, but "signs" of the approaching sovereignty of God in its attack upon the counterforces of demonic alienation. As such they do not silence their addressees and witnesses. They do not set them under tutelage, as sorcery and magic do, but they address them, and draw them into the liberating history of the kingdom of God. It is a striking thing how again and again in connection with the miracle stories the question of personal faith is raised and the readiness for discipleship is awakened. The power of Jesus is manifestly a power that addresses and empowers us in personal ways.

This aspect is underlined by the fact that according to the testimony of the New Testament the power of Jesus does not manifest itself merely in spectacular outward acts, but also, and surely above all, as the authority of his *word*. Accordingly, his power illumines and sets in motion "from within." The astonishment of the people applies not only to the acts of power but also to the impressive teaching. It is surely no accident that at the end of the Sermon on the Mount, Matthew summarizes the impression of the people by saying: "Unlike their own teachers he taught with a note of authority" (Matt. 7: 29). Not only the miracles, but also, for example, the parables are plain enough signs of the nearness and meaning of the kingdom of God.

The "last word" on the New Testament understanding of the power of God in its connection with the event of Christ is provided by the *Easter story:* his cross and his resurrection. The *raising* of the cruficied Christ is according to the unanimous testimony of the New Testament the final and decisive revelation of the power of God. The question of what the power of God is, and indeed who God himself is, receives its answer from here. One of the most frequently employed formulas of confession is the affirmation of him "who raised Jesus our Lord from the dead" (Rom. 4: 24 etc.). Consequently, it is with this event that the power of God, too, is identified and "defined" (cf. 1 Cor.

6: 14; 2 Cor. 13: 4; Rom. 1: 4 etc.). It is the "power of an indestructible life" (Heb. 7: 16) that triumphed at Easter over death and its consorts, the powers of sin and alienation.

In this context, in the light of the resurrection, the *cross* must on no account be left out: the power of God acknowledges the powerlessness of the crucified Christ. It is a striking thing that when Paul with his eye on Jesus Christ speaks of the "power of God," he points precisely to the crucifixion: "We proclaim Christ nailed to the cross; and though this is a stumbling block to Jews and folly to Greeks, yet to those who have heard his call, Jews and Greeks alike, he is the power of God and the wisdom of God" (1 Cor. 1: 23f.). It is here, at the cross of Jesus, that for Paul and for the whole new Testament the ultimate "revaluation of all values" takes place; to put it quite pointedly in our context: the "revolution in the concept of power." The power of God does not exclude human powerlessness, but encompasses it, absorbs it. It is the power that is strong in weakness, the power of love giving and sacrificing itself for others, such love as was maintained and verified to the end by the Man of Nazareth. It is *this* love that proves itself on Easter morning to be stronger than death: the true "power of an indestructible life," the power of God in the eminent sense, is the *love of Christ*.

It is to this power that Christians appeal and it is this power that they confess when they pray: "Thine is the power." Does this bring about any change in the power relationships in our world?

The Power of the Powerless

I should like to introduce my reflections on this difficult question by means of two quotations. They are statements by two thinkers to whom I am particularly indebted philosophically and theologically. The two did not know each other. However at different places during the years of the last world war they both wrestled as Christians with the same question, with our question: how does God work in a power-possessed world?

In 1942, when seriously ill, the Czech philosopher *Emanuel Radl* derived from the gospel a "daringly risky answer," namely, that "God acts as Christ acted; that he compels no one, that God is accordingly a completely defenseless being; that he performs no miracles, that he sends neither lightning nor flood nor plague upon men; that he does not punish men upon this earth, that he does not directly protect the wheat from the tares. . . . He works as Christ worked: he bears all things, even crucifixion; yet he loves men above all things and accordingly helps in the way defenseless people do: he teaches, guides, commends, gives examples, exhorts, warns. And what sort of method does he choose? He sends out good men, who . . . like angels of God set an example, guide, exhort, warn" (*Utěcha z filosofie,* p. 23).

A little later, when in prison, *Dietrich Bonhoeffer* said on a similar subject: "God would have us know that we must live as men who manage our lives without him. . . . God lets himself be pushed out of the world on to the cross. He is weak and powerless in the world, and that is precisely the way, the only way, in which he is with us and helps us. . . . The Bible points man to the powerlessness and suffering of God . . . who gains power and place in the world by his weakness" (*Widerstand und Ergebung,* p. 241f., ed. by R.H. Fuller; *Letters and Papers from Prison,* 1953, p. 163f.; 3rd ed. revised by F. Clarke, 1967, p. 196).

These are certainly impressive, stirring, in part also irritating and disputable testimonies. The power of God appears (especially in Radl's case) to have been withdrawn from the world of earthly affairs. A capitulation? A projection of our own feelings of impotence, a resignation and accommodation to the prevailing power relationships? In view of the pandemonium of power beyond the writers' door and their own powerlessness in sickbay and prison cell, these would humanly speaking be completely understandable reactions.

Yet it would be a profound misunderstanding to interpret the thinking of Radl and Bonhoeffer in such a defeatist sense. A simple argument against this interpretation is the course of two thinkers' lives: Radl was a philosopher for whom personal involvement in the cause of truth and justice was one of the decisive criteria of philosophical existence. Bonhoeffer set the seal to his discipleship of Christ as a member of the Resistance against Nazism. Incidentally, in the immediate context of both quotations there are references that point in a totally different direction to that of resignation. There can surely be no misunderstanding Bonhoeffer's remark about God as one "who gains power and place in the world by his weakness." Bonhoeffer is accordingly very much concerned with "power and place in the world," not at all with passive renunciation of the world and its dismissal from the realm of our responsibility. And in Radl's case we find at the end of the chapter on the "defenseless moral world" the following words: "Defenseless culture—I am seized by the holy enthusiasm which I experienced as a youth in a church full of people in festive garments—and all of us, all of us, sang till the windows rattled and the walls trembled from the fulness of pious awe: 'Mighty God, thy name we bless!' " (op. cit., p. 24).

I understand Radl and Bonhoeffer rather as witnesses to that "revolution in the concept of power" that was fulfilled in the history and destiny of Jesus Christ. Both of them take seriously the Christians' daily prayer: "Thine is the power!" In so doing they have no illusions concerning the "real power relationships": in terms of power politics it was surely brutally plain in Nazi-occupied Prague and in the Nazi prison in Berlin where the power lies. The power aggregates of the overlords had the two witnesses in their hands, and not only brushed the margin of their lives, but broke them. Radl and Bonhoeffer did not reconcile themselves to this, but combatted the "real power" in order to gain "more room" also in the political sense for themselves and their fellowmen. In this they failed. Remember that four days after Bonhoeffer had written the letter from which we have quoted, the attempt to remove Hitler failed and he knew very well that this would now presumably mean death also for him. The final solution of the problem of power? Bonhoeffer sees it otherwise. On the day of the failure he writes a poem, the third verse of which takes up our question and gives it a central place:

Suffering

O wondrous change! Those hands, once so strong and active, have now been bound. Helpless and forlorn, you see the end of your deed. Yet with a sigh of relief you resign your cause to a stronger hand, and are content to do so. For one brief moment you enjoyed the bliss of freedom, only to give it back to God, that he might perfect it in glory.

These words of Bonhoeffer's make it plainly evident what it means to pray the doxology of the Lord's Prayer, "Thine is the power," realistically in the midst of prevailing power relationships. The doors of the prison do not open—not always, at any rate, and not at once. Yet they do not have their victim ultimately in hand. Our life is "in a stronger hand" than the merciless hands of the power aggregates. Thine is the power: hence it is possible even in the stifling atmosphere of the prison cell to "draw a new breath." When new breath is thus drawn by free men and women, there, even in situations of powerlessness, "place and power" are gained—a bridgehead of the kingdom of God amid the realm of the powers. The power of the powerless.

A "wondrous transformation" is thus given to the question of power in the perspective of the confession, "Thine is the power." What is power? The question can of course be answered, for example, in the sense of Stalin's notorious counterquestion: "How many divisions does the Pope have?" Less cynical practical politicians also tend to give to human questions, above all to political problems, an answer purely in terms of massive power. From their point-of-view they are right, too. The course of history, at any rate, hardly contradicts them. When God is left out from the start and the kingdom of God is packed off into the realm of illusion, then power positivism seems to be the answer readiest at hand. Here, however, the prayer of Jesus intrudes itself. The gospel, to recall Radl, has a different, "daringly risky answer": true power, the power to which the future belongs, is the power of the history of Jesus: the power of love. This power finds it heavy going in the world of the powers—just as Jesus himself found it heavy going. It is, however, since Easter morning, ultimately superior to them. And this, too, not just at the "last day," but already today: this power alone gives human life and also human history their true, abiding meaning. This, too, can surely, with open eyes, be learned from history here and there. Powers and lords come and go—the seemingly most powerful are often the ones that go the quickest and the most shamefully. Love, on the contrary, as Paul says, "never comes to an end" (1 Cor. 13: 8). It alone is the "power of an indestructible life."

Here the general problem of power changes into an *"argumentum ad hominem,"* a question addressed personally to each of us: What is your view of power? What is your point of orientation in your ethical and political decisions? To whom do you ascribe the ultimate power over yourself and your society —and this not merely theoretically or in solemn declarations, but in practice, in your everyday decisions, in determining your priorities? The established power complexes and power constellations in every society tend to "relieve" their citizens of their decisions. They tend to regard the existing state of power without more ado as the best and the only real one. In particularly massive form, we see an example in the authoritarianly administered "real socialism" of the East European sort with its monopoly of power and truth in the hands of one party. More subtly, however, in Western society the economic "structural constraints" are developed and manipulated. Every search for alternatives is discredited as being "naïve," if not indeed denounced as a lapse into chaos and anarchy. Thus the *status quo* of power becomes a tabu and a fetish.

The prayer of Jesus, "Thine is the power," contradicts the positivistic and fetishistic power systems. It refers to that power which provides the alternative to all earthly authorities however glorious their appearance. Existing powers are thereby not indeed denied their power—the latter is taken completely seriously even in the eschatological perspective (think, for example, of Rom. 13)—but they *are* denied all "omnipotence." Where the power of God is recalled, there it is known that what is real in our human world is not merely the existing power relationships, but also that power which does not lie at our disposal, yet is placed at our disposal in the Spirit of Jesus, namely, the power of the love of Christ. On this we can and must take our bearings in faith. Thus there arises in the world of people, by the name and the power of God, a "free place" that cannot be ultimately blocked by the constraints of any power. It is the open, urgent, very pertinent task of "good people" (of whom Radl spoke). It is above all the task of Christians to take over this place that has been authoritatively gained by the powerlessness of God and to fill it in discipleship.

To this task we now turn our attention in closing. Two themes may serve to give it more concrete shape: "the demythologizing of power" and "love and grace."

The De-mythologizing of Power

We return to the statements of Nietzsche and Burckhardt on the subject of power, as quoted at the beginning. Despite contrary evaluations of the phenomenon, the two writers agree in one important point: they diagnose in human struggle for power a tendency towards "more and more power," towards "supremacy" (Nietzsche), "a lust . . . to increase itself" (Burckhardt). The experiences of history confirm this judgment, more especially in our century, with drastic plainness. The insatiable lust for supremacy leads to ever new catastrophes—and not only in the military sense. Here we have a challenge to Christian theology. It has to unmask this tendency, to draw attention to it and to work resolutely against it. In doing so, theology need not simply take over Burckhardt's sweeping judgment: it is not the case that "power is evil in itself, no matter who exercises it." There is such a thing as legitimate power, namely, opportunity and right of human beings as individuals and as a society, despite all alien determination by nature or society, to become the subject of their own destinies. Thus in political life, too, we have not simply to strive after the "abolition" of power, but rather for its "redistribution," in constant commitment to the task of increasing the chances of life for the powerless. Yet we can never be critical enough of the notorious temptations of power.

Here *biblical outlook* can be a help to the church and to society. It is surely striking how sharply the prophetic message criticizes autocratic power—and this, too, both in its underlying anthropological foundation (think, for example, of the story of the Fall and of that of the Tower of Babel), and also in view of concrete historical manifestations of the lust for power. The dream of omnipotence is found to be a sinful misunderstanding of human condition and shown to be destructive and self-destructive. The prophets and apostles accordingly "demythologize" this dream and urge us to take a sober and critical attitude towards power. Again and again, often in vehement polemic, they proclaim the alternative, in order to rouse people out of the deadly intoxication of limited power. The church, above all, is summoned to a clear decision: the Christians in particular must bear in mind that other power, the power of God and testify to it in word and conduct. "Neither by force of arms nor by brute strength, but by my spirit! says the Lord of hosts" (Zech. 4: 6; cf. also Ps. 33: 16–18; Ps. 20: 8; Prov. 21: 31 etc.). And in the New Testament, in the Magnificat, the story of Jesus is announced right from the start to be the manifestation of the power of God in opposition to all the autocratic power of the lords of the earth: "The deeds his own right arm has done disclose his might: the arrogant of heart and mind he has put to rout, he has brought down monarchs from their thrones, but the humble have been lifted high" (Luke 1: 51f.). There can be no doubt that the praise of the power of God (and also our doxology!) has a critical edge to it. The essential human issues cannot be solved by oppressive force—and vice versa: the oppressive power is helpless in solving the essential human issues.

In positive elaboration of the "de-mythologizing of power" we must point out the *significance of law.* Law is a human expedient and a human attempt to set limits to the arbitrariness of power. To be sure, it is often only a fragile expedient that can all too easily be blunted or misused—a dam that is repeatedly pierced and broken through by the pent-up streams of power. No wonder the significance of law is today disparaged on the right and the left, by authoritarian and anti-authoritarian movements. Christian theology ought not to join in underestimating law. The dam, despite its fragility and in all its fragility, must be built with perseverence.

Once again the biblical outlook can be a help to us in this task. "The holy scriptures never speak of God's power . . . in abstraction from the concept of law: the power of God is essentially the power of law. It is no mere *potentia,* but *potestas,* that is to say: legitimate power, founded upon law" (K. Barth, *Dogmatik im Grundriss,* 4th ed., p. 55). I recall our reflections on the Old Testament view of power: as revealed in the event of the exodus, God's power aims at the founding of the covenant, the legal constituting of the people of God. It is no "absolute" power resting in itself, but a "relative" power oriented towards the covenant partner and his right to live. In this sense it can be said that in the social and political realm the biblical view of power calls for a "democratic," not an "autocratic" exercise of power.

Christian churches have largely failed to pass these biblical impulses on to their society, above all in the German-speaking area. Gustav Heinemann, a statesman and a confessing Christian, is right when he points out that "our democratic state" has grown up "without Christian initiative" and that in this sphere German theology has a great deal to make up. In the Anglosaxon and Swiss (and also the Czech) area the balance may be more positive. I think, for example, of the theological efforts of a Reinhold Niebuhr or a Karl Barth. The Christian church in all areas, however, has the important task of working out biblical theology's contribution to the questions concerned with power and law. This remains an open and, in view of the increasing dangers of power, very pertinent task. In this respect the church should not leave its society in the lurch, nor theology fail the social sciences.

A stimulating contribution in this direction was recently made by the Swiss theologian *Arthur Rich* in his booklet, *Radikalitat und Rechtsstaatlichkeit* (1978). Rich is convinced that from the standpoint of the biblical understanding of God all "monocratic" models of power have to be fundamentally called into question. He points in this context to the hitherto unexhausted significance of the trinitarian dogma: if the highest power in the trinitarian sense is to be understood as "God the Father, the Son and the Holy Spirit," then it is not a "monological" but a "dialogical" power. It introduces us into "the sphere of righteous power, the purpose of which is precisely not to disempower the subordinate party, but to give him a share in its own power. The notion of the participative reigning of believers along with God (2 Tim. 2: 12) has its foundation here" (*op. cit.,* p. 34). This concept is analagous to the constitutional ideas of the necessary limitation of power by the separation of the legislative, executive and juridical authorities, to which, for example, the Swiss professor of constitutional law, Max Imboden, has drawn attention. (This analogy is no accident.) From the standpoint of the Christian understanding of God, at all events, we have to strive after an effective "de-mythologizing of power."

The Power of Love, the Power of Grace

The task of the de-mythologizing of power in the light of the prayer, "Thine is the power," must never be under-estimated. Yet the decisive contribution which the church can make to its society in the midst of the constraints of power is the witness and the initiative of *love.* It is surely in this direction that our doxology and the whole message of the New Testament plainly point. Let us remember that the final New Testament word on the subject of the power of God is the reference to the crucified and risen Lord—that is, to the love of Jesus Christ. This love is the ultimate power. It is accordingly the cardinal point for guiding the believer in the world of the powers. This love has lived and suffered before our eyes in the life of Jesus. It has found impressive articulation in his teaching, above all surely in the Sermon on the Mount and in the double Commandment of Love. It has now to be followed.

The effectiveness and the binding character of the love of Jesus in the realm of power politics has often been doubted.

"One cannot govern the world by means of the Sermon on the Mount," is an oft-repeated saying of political realists. And theological realists agree with this in principle: the commandment of love points to an "impossible possibility" (Reinhold Niebuhr) in the world of the powers. The realists have arguments in their favor that have to be taken seriously. We cannot turn the love and the commandment of Christ immediately, legally, fanatically into a political program. The power of God is not given over to our management. It does not stand at our disposal. Yet we can put ourselves at the disposal of the power of God. We can take the love of Christ as our orientation point, and we can move in its direction in our thought and action.

No doubt there is a danger of sentimentalism in much of the traditional religious love talk. It aspires toward the heavenly heights of pure ideas and does not reach the lows of earthly material conditions. However, the love in the sense of the New Testament is different. It is the "incarnational love" oriented towards the human world in its concrete needs of body, soul, and spirit. With good reason, the ecumenical social ethics has been emphasizing "the love working through structures," encouraging the transfer, step by step, of the initiatives of love into measures aiming at less injustice and more justice.

The Indian economist, S. L. Parmar, puts it in the following words: "Structures of injustice are immune to sentimental invocations. Power can express love, only if it promotes justice. The first step in developing such power is to oppose injustice. The prophetic admonition: 'Let justice flow down like waters,' and Christ's teaching: 'Love your neighbor as yourself,' are integral parts of the power that is needed. Inherent in these calls is the challenge to existing injustice in relations, institutions and values." ("Application of the Christian Concept of Power to the Social Order," p. 34, in *Society and Religion,* ed. by R.W. Taylor Madras, 1976).

It is this movement of discipleship that counts—also, precisely, in the political realm. We have noted that power without law becomes boundless, destructive, and self-destructive. Now, however, we must also say that law without love is in danger of turning rigid, of becoming lovelessness and mercilessness. *"Summum ius—summa iniuria,"* said the Romans with their eye on this danger. Thus the open horizon of a love that presses for "greater righteousness" (in the sense of the Sermon on the Mount and of Jesus' commandment of love) is in the interest of law, and ultimately also of the political strategy for the limitation of power. Christians must already for this reason stand unmistakably in their society for the power of Jesus: in word and deed, in the persistent search for new possibilities in the removal of all personal and structural lovelessness. The salt of the commandments and promises of Jesus is needed not only by the church but also by society. The worlds of power and of law require for their fermentation processes the leaven of love.

And they require the light of *grace.* Grace and love in the gospel belong very closely together. They are often, for example by the apostle Paul, mentioned together in one breath as the sum of the saving history of Christ. "The grace of our Lord Jesus Christ, the love of God." The power of love is understood in the new Testament to be the power of grace. Yet the two words set their own specific accents.

It is not easy for us today to make the specific point of the biblical concept of grace understandable. All too often grace has been mediated in church circles as "cheap grace," consoling with pious hopes, "opium of the people" (K. Marx). In the dialogue between Christians and Marxists a credible interpretation of the biblical message of grace has therefore been one of the most difficult tasks. At the same time, however, it is also one of the most essential. For when rightly understood, it is precisely the "foreign" accent of the word "grace" that is particularly important in the context of modern life in East and West. Grace points unmistakably to the *limits of the makeable.* It does not underestimate one's works. Grace in the biblical sense means not the tranquilizing but rather the mobilizing of humanity. But grace reminds us that the ultimate in our life, our ultimate rights and righteousness, are not of our own achieving. The salvation and happiness of people are not makeable. Yet they are not for that reason "sour grapes" on the tree of life, hanging too high. They are in the midst of our life—as the offer of grace.

This positive factor of grace holds liberating significance precisely in the context of the question of power. Is it not the case that behind the pernicious urge and constraint of power towards supremacy, behind this destructive and self-destructive madness, there ultimately lies the false belief that our life and salvation are to be secured by power of making and making of power? Is not the mercilessness of the makers—and of the technocratic or ideological, capitalistic or "real socialist" systems administered by them—is not this our great danger? The biblical message of grace breaks through the mechanisms of making and of power—seeks the human persons avalanched behind them and gives them back their God-created soul: "For what does it profit a man, if he gain the whole world and lose his own soul?" (Mark 8: 36). This was and this is the way of Jesus: grace is the triumph of his love over the gracelessness of hearts and conditions. It is the privilege of Christians to bear witness to this triumph of grace: in divine worship, in interhuman relationships, but also in persistent advocacy of grace in the social sphere (think of the realm of education, social welfare or penal justice). Not salvation by power, but the power of salvation is our hope. *"For thine is the power."*

III
THINE
IS THE
GLORY

The Glory of God
and Our Human Future

A Dubious Triumphalism?

Thine is the glory: it is the final word of our sentence which provides its traditional name of *doxology*. "Doxa" is the Greek expression for glory. This very fact suggests that the ultimate intention and confession of the Lord's Prayer culminates in this final word. In particular, the Reformed Tradition highlighted its paramount importance: *Soli Deo Gloria*— to God alone be the glory—has always been its principle and program for thought and life.

The content and the meaning of the term can be easily misunderstood today. "Glory," "Glorius," "Glorification"— these concepts seem to breathe the spirit of *triumphalism*. Such a spirit would be a flat contradiction to the integrity and credibility of the gospel. When the World Alliance of Reformed Churches was engaged in preparations for its 1977 Centennial Consultation under the general theme, "The Glory of God and the Future of Man," there were indeed doubts and even protests from theologians, particularly on the North American Continent. They warned us: You Reformed people do not fall prey to the temptation of triumphalism and imperialism so often connected with the Reformed tradition especially in its Anglo-American version!

Such voices are to be taken seriously. *"Theologia gloriae,"* that is, a one-sided emphasis on the "glorious" aspects of our faith (in opposition to a "Theologia Crucis"), is a problematic undertaking both theologically and ecclesiastically. Does our prayer "Thine is the glory" point in such a dubious direction? Here a careful theological analysis of the biblical concept of the glory becomes important.

The Glory of God in the Biblical View

It is not only for reasons of loyalty to the formal principle of the Reformation, *Sola Scriptura,* but also for special and very concrete reasons that we begin our consideration of the "glory of God" biblically. The New Testament expression for "glory," *doxa,* although derived from general Greek usage, has its specific biblical meaning which cannot be understood from the Greek background alone. In that background, *doxa* means "opinion." This meaning in its subjective sense, "my opinion," has totally disappeared, and in the objective sense, "an opinion about me," it is only weakly attested. "In the NT, however, the word is used for the most part in a sense for which there is no Greek analogy whatever. . . . That is to say, it denotes 'divine and heavenly radiance,' the 'loftiness and majesty' of God, and even the 'being of God' and His world" (Kittel, *TDNT,* II, p. 237). This usage can only be understood in terms of the Old Testament.

The Hebrew expression which is translated in the Septuagint with *doxa* is *kabod.* It is rooted in profane usage: the glory of a person consists of his "weight," his respect, his prestige in his position of honor within his society. The "glory of the Lord" is established in a similar fashion: it expresses the power, sublimity, and beauty of Yahweh. In its theological usage, the term is notably enriched, deepened, and concretized.

The approach is very vivid—many of the descriptions of the glory of Yahweh (e.g., Ps. 97:1f.; Exod. 24:15f.; Exod. 1:1f.) are reminiscent in their terminology of weather phenomena—fire, lightning, storm, and clouds. But they are not focusing on meteorological phenomena as such and they do not represent simply the traces of a "weather god religion." The theological conclusions to be drawn from this approach lead in another direction. I would like to point out four central emphases.

1. *The radiant "glory of the Lord" signals the special nearness of the unapproachable God in his revelation.* At several key passages, the glory of God accompanies the revelation event in the Old Testament (Exod. 24:15f.; Isa. 6; Ezek. 1:1f.). It is exceptionally appropriate for this. The glory makes a dialectic clear which is typical for the biblical witness to God: it demonstrates both the incomprehensibility and the nearness of Yahweh simultaneously. Yahweh is the free and sublime God. His glory is like a devouring fire (Exod. 24:17), and to see God is to die (Exod. 33:20f.). There is no sense in which we can control God. He cannot be captured in images nor bound to cultic installations. His glory can even depart from the legitimate holy place, the temple. But this unapproachable and uncontrollable God is not an alien and distant God. He reveals himself in the midst of his people, and manifests his glory in nearness. The One who cannot be controlled can be intimate.

2. *The glory of God encounters Israel in its history.* "The incomparable power of Yahweh is also experienced in history, wherever Yahweh 'gets himself glory' (Exod. 14:4, 17f.; Ezek. 28:22), that is where the power of his action in history becomes apparent" (G. von Rad, *Theology of the Old Testament*, pp. 239–240). Yahweh reveals himself as the Lord of history. Not only the heavens, but also the earth belongs to him. In the light of his glory, the glory of earthly rulers and orders pales; they are "de-deified." Even Pharaoh must submit. Thus the history of the people of God is qualified as a history of liberation. In

this regard, the Exodus is ascribed key significance (Num. 14:22). And it is thus understandable that in the praise of the glory of God, constant mention is made of "his righteousness" (Ps. 97:6) and of "his handiwork" (Ps. 19:1).

3. *The theological center of this liberating presence of God in the history of his people is the Covenant.* God's glory is not a *"mysterium tremendum"* without theological contours or ethical obligations. It seeks the relationship between God and humanity which is defined in the Covenant, the relationship of faith and loyalty as it is articulated in the commands of the decalogue within the setting of the Exodus. The glory is at once liberating and obligating. It is quite noticeable how closely knit the glory of God is with the Covenant events. We think immediately of the solemn conclusion of the Covenant on Sinai: it reaches its culmination in the revelation of the glory of God (Exod. 24:15f.). And later, in close connection with the ark of the covenant (1 Sam. 4:22), it appears in those critical hours of the history of the Covenant, such as in the dramatic events which are described in Numbers 13 and 14. In its appearance, the whole betrayal committed by the Covenant-breaking people is subjected to judgment, and yet in spite of that, the unbroken, and even unbreakable Covenant loyalty of Yahweh is emphasized. If I see it properly, this is the direction in which the innermost theological core of the "glory of God" is to be sought. God's honor does not revolve around itself. The glory and honor of God are his loyalty and faithfulness. His glory is directed towards the people. It seals the eternal Covenant.

4. *As a demonstration of the special nearness and loyalty of Yahweh, the glory of God illumines the future of Israel and the future of the nations.* The *kabod* of Yahweh is revelant to the present situation of the people of God, but, in view of the majesty of the Lord of history, it breaks through this present situation and opens the way towards hope. In this way, Israel is given a future. Its historical pilgrimage is not meaningless

and goalless. Israel is not a blind nomadic people, underway "to nowhere." Israel is the "wandering people of God," underway to the messianic goal established and promised in the Covenant. The ideas and concepts which are connected to this goal, which is called in the New Testament the kingdom of God, are many-sided and variable. It is important for our context that in all of this an important role is ascribed to the glory of God. It receives its *eschatological dimension.* And conversely, the eschatological future is molded by the glory of God. The Old Testament witnesses even dare to characterize the messianic future as the age of glory. This reveals a special kind of dynamic. In this moving hope for the glory of God, walls and boundaries are burst open, even those between the people of God and the other nations. The ultimate revelation of the glory of God applies to everyone (Isa. 40:5; Ezek. 39:21) and illuminates the whole earth. The glory of God *is* the future of the nations.

The Glory of God in Jesus Christ

There is no break in the understanding of the "glory of God" in the transition from the Old to the New Testaments. There is, however, a radical step in making it concrete. There is no break: *doxa* is a valid rendering of *kabod.* The basic lines of the messages of the glory of God remain the same. In the New Testament too, the *doxa* signals the nearness of God in his revelation. It is related to the new people of God in the "fulness of time," in the midst of history. It becomes the seal of the new and insurpassable covenant. And it has its eschatological and dynamic orientation: the kingdom of God is the kingdom of glory. The continuity between the two Testaments is at this particular point especially strong.

Yet, the New Testament brings a unique kind of concretization. It brings it not just in regard to the predicates of the glory of God but to its very subject. The word which has become the "bearer of the message of God" now is made into

the "bearer of the message of Christ." The attribution of *doxa*
to God—"glory to God in the highest" (Luke 2:14; 19:38; Rev.
4:9) finds parallels in relation to Christ (Heb. 13:21; 1 Pet. 4:11;
Rev. 5:12f.). Alongside the "God of glory" of Acts 7:2 we may
set the "Lord of glory" of 1 Cor. 2:8; James 2:1. If OT eschatology implies: "seeing the glory of the Lord," Isaiah 40:5,
NT eschatology implies: "the appearing of the glory of our
great God and savior Christ Jesus" (Tit. 2:13) (Kittel, *TDNT,*
II, p. 248). It could be said that the whole person and history
of Jesus Christ are surrounded and accompanied by the glory
of God. And conversely, the whole person and history of Jesus
Christ are an exposition of the "glory of God." I would like to
deal with both aspects of this central New Testament understanding.

Most of the New Testament statements about the glory of
Christ refer to the post-Easter history, to his resurrection and
parousia. The references given above all point in this direction,
and this accent could be strengthened from virtually every book
in the New Testament. It is the Resurrected One who is linked
with the glory of God (Rom. 6:4; 1 Pet. 1:21; 1 Tim. 3:16; Acts
7:55). And it is the coming Son of Man who has his disposal
"great power and glory" (Mark 13:26; 8:38; 10:37; 13:26; Matt.
19:28; 25:31). *Doxa* is not less eschatological in thrust than
kabod.

But this eschatology is inextricably intertwined with the
earthly history of Jesus of Nazareth. To be sure, the word *doxa*
is only used in regard to the earthly in a hesitating fashion,
especially in the terminology of the synoptics. The unab-
breviated and unadorned humanity of the person of Jesus may
not be disregarded, retouched, or even explained away. But it
is in the very humanity of Jesus that, according to the witness
of the New Testament, the final revelation of the glory of God
takes place. The synoptic evangelists imply this at several essential boundary marks in their accounts. One example would be

Luke in his Christmas story, where the whole life of Jesus is placed under the angel's statements in which the glory of God is linked with earthly peace. And all of the synoptics include in the middle of their accounts the "transfiguration" (Mark 9:2–10; Matt. 17:1–9; Luke 9:28–36).

This story deserves special attention in our context. It is an especially evocative testimony to the concealed character of the presence of the glory of God in the earthly life of Jesus. The glory appears here in a mysterious incident upon the countenance of Christ. The inner circle of disciples is both terrified and fascinated. They want to settle down upon the mount of transfiguration. But one cannot "keep" the glory of God, one cannot bathe in its radiance. The story points beyond itself, establishes relationships backwards to the Old Testament event of Sinai, and forwards to the resurrection and second coming. But above all, this revelation "in the heights" points directly and unmistakably to "the depths": the suffering of Jesus Christ is announced, and the disciples are immediately confronted with the concrete human suffering as this story concludes (Mark 9:14–29 par.).

This conclusion of the story of the transfiguration reveals the other and decisive element of the New Testament witness to the glory in Jesus Christ. This glory is connected with the suffering of Jesus, and thus it is properly related to the situations of human suffering. Here we come upon the central statement of the New Testament: God reveals his glory in the cross of Jesus. This view is established in the scopus of the synoptic gospels, in their witness to the suffering Son of Man. And it becomes explicitly and openly the basic thrust of the Johannine message of glory: the way of exaltation is the way of the cross. "The *doxa* derives from His death. At the same time, what Jesus does in His passion is a process through which 'God is glorified in Him' (John 13:31)" (Kittel, *TDNT,* II, p. 249). Paul sees the relationship no less clearly: the "Lord of glory" is the

Crucified One (1 Cor. 2:8). In the prism of the glory of God, with which the New Testament witnesses attest to Jesus Christ, his cross is not excluded but shifted into the center. The cross is the sign and the ground of his glory.

What may we conclude from this integral connection of our Christian understanding of the glory of God—with the person and history of Jesus Christ and thus with our whole theme? In continuity with the three basic aspects of the gospel history I would like to stress primarily three accents.

1. *The glory of God in Jesus Christ is glory with a human face.* Both motifs in this statements are to be taken seriously, even the word *"face."* In one of the most important passages on glory, Paul speaks of "the glory of God in the face of Christ" (2 Cor. 4:6). This removes any magical overtones to our discussion of glory and broadly personalizes it. "God's glory is the glory of His face, indeed His face itself, God in person, God who bears a name, and calls us by name" (K. Barth, *C.D.,* II, 1, p. 647). And it is glory with a *human* face. Its way is that of the incarnation, as it is bindingly exposed in the history of the man from Nazareth. In his spirit it is not a "glory" which "rules from above" but a glory which "serves from below" (Phil. 2:5–11). It does not blind the senses but moves the heart. It does not seek out people in order to confound them or to "unmask" them and to strip them bare, but to take them up and set them aright. It is the glory of *humane love.*

2. *The glory of God in Jesus Christ is the glory of the cross (gloria crucis).* This definition is to be grasped very precisely. It does not by any means glorify suffering in general, it is not an affirmation of masochistic or sadistic tendencies. It is related to the cross of Jesus Christ. It praises the love of God which is stronger than death. *This* love is the glory of the cross. God reveals himself in it. This is the New Testament "re-valuation of all values" which also applies to the concept of "glory." The fact that this glory of God is relevant to oppressed and suffering

people is not something new in the New Testament but already a part of the Old Testament understanding of the covenant glory of God. But the assertion that this glory not only encompasses suffering but actually reveals its essence in suffering, the suffering of God, is the real "revolution" in the New Testament understanding of doxa.

This revaluation has important theological consequences:

> The view that God is glorious in contrast to all that is lowly is proved to be false and pagan by the fact that "though he was rich, yet for your sake he became poor" (2 Cor. 8:9). The divine omnipotence (as distinguished from all abstract conceptions of power) is just that it can assume the form of the weakness and helplessness of the man on the Cross, and in that form can triumph. God does not forfeit his glory or lay it aside when He assumes the form of a servant. On the contrary, He confirms it. In the humiliation of the Son of God, God is truly glorious in contrast to the loveless glory of all the gods invented by men (A.C. Cochrane, *The Glory of God*).

3. *The glory of God in Jesus Christ is demonstrated in the power of his resurrection as the power of the new in the midst of the old.* We saw that the most explicit statements about the glory of Christ are related to his resurrection and his parousia. These are eschatological events. They belong to the new world of God. But these events break into our time. (If Christ "has been resurrected into the glory of the coming God, then conversely this glory comes in Him and through His history into the misery of this age" (J. Moltmann, in *Evangelische Theologie,* 1975, p. 216). The "powers of the age to come" (Heb. 6:5) are set free and empower us humans to risk the new in our history. The world of man has been "de-fatalized." The rising of Christ inaugurates the "uprising" of the children of God, more concretely, the Christian mission into "all the world." The glory of God both finds and mobilizes its witnesses.

The Glory of God in the Church

We are not here and now excluded from the glory of God. But the form in which we are surrounded by it, and in which we participate in it, is the form of the Church" (K. Barth, *C.D.*, II, 1, p. 676). The concrete focus of *doxa* in the church corresponds to the Christological in the New Testament: the glory of God has its concrete social location. It does not appear abstractly between heaven and earth and is not a *"theatrum magicum."* It does not evaporate into abstract generalities nor into abstract individualism. It summons forth a definite human community: the church.

It is remarkable to see with what matter-of-factness the New Testament message of the glory of God is applied to the very concrete situation of the Christian congregations. The emphatic "we" of the Apostolic witness cannot be ignored at this point. The strong factor of participation permeates the New Testament praise of the glory of God. Christ did not die for himself and rise from the dead for himself, but for many—more explicitly, for us. Therefore we already participate in his glory. "The glory of Christ illuminates the earthly existence of Christians as a whole, it stands under the radiance of that glory (2 Cor. 3:18), precisely at the place where the Christian is made into the 'refuse of the world' (1 Cor. 4:9f.), 'sometimes being publicly exposed to abuse and affliction' (Heb. 10:33)" (H.U. von Balthasar, *Herrlichkeit,* III, 2, 339). Christians are the people of glory.

Does this view of the church imply some kind of enthusiastic triumphalism? Doubtless the church in its history is constantly tempted to exploit the witness to the glory in a triumphalistic way. But that is then one of the most dangerous misunderstandings of the church—and a profound misunderstanding of the biblical view of glory. Let us remember that the glory of Christ is the glory of the cross. Then, of necessity, the "people of glory" is not a "glorious people," but the people under the cross. The apostolic witness to our participation in this glory permits no doubts at this point. Again and again the tension between our participation in the cross and the resurrection is testified to. Constantly our life, too, is drawn into this tension. There is no tensionless, "smooth" Christian existence from the point-of-view of the glory of God.

This is expressed with special clarity by Paul in 2 Corinthians 4. This passage is a strong witness to the glory of God in the life of the Christian. "But we have this treasure in earthen vessels. . . . We are afflicted in every way, but not crushed; perplexed, but not driven to despair; persecuted, but not forsaken; struck down, but not destroyed; always carrying in the body the death of Jesus, so that the life of Jesus may also be manifested in our bodies" (vss. 7–10). The whole drama of Christian existence is described in these sentences. We have not yet reached the goal but remain underway. The glory of the church is not self-glory. It is "broken glory."

However, the drama of Christian existence is not a blind fate of tragedy. It would be completely wrong to interpret the ambiguity and brokenness of the Christian life in terms of a permanent "tied score." The score is not fifty-fifty between the cross and the resurrection. There is no "balance of terror" here but the dynamic of hope. The old is passing away, and the new is coming. The tension of glory has an eschatological thrust, towards promise, towards hope, towards the kingdom of God. Thus the same Paul who knows so clearly and profoundly the misery of the church and his own misery can place the life of the Christian beneath the promise of a movement from "one degree of glory to another" (2 Cor. 3:18).

This bold step is based, however, upon only one thing. The Apostle immediately names it: the presence of the Spirit. The

confidence of the church can never be based upon the idea that
"ultimately it will manage," that the "holy elements" in it will
eventually assert themselves. The superiority of glory over the
power of "our afflictions" (2 Cor. 4:14) is not based upon
our potentiality but is given in the actuality of the Holy Spirit.
"The Spirit helps us in our weakness" (Rom. 8:26): that is
both the promise and the experience of the Christian. And thus
the "freedom of the children of God" is already granted in the
conditions of what is (yet) manifold slavery and alienation. The
Spirit of Christ who is the Spirit of freedom breaks through all
the "tied scores" and hopeless situations of life and sets us in
motion again "towards hope" (cf. Rom. 8:21). In him the glory
of the church is grounded and experienced.

The result of this grounding is that "the glory of God in
the church" may never be merely admired as a legacy nor held
on to as a possession but must be witnessed to and verified. As
it is made concrete in Jesus Christ, it demands the correspond-
ingly concrete response of the Christians. Its scope encompasses all areas of the church's life, just as the incarnation of
God in Christ encompasses all areas of human life. I would like
to emphasize three dimensions of this response.

1. I will begin with the *evangelistic and missionary* dimension. At the beginning of this section I quoted Karl Barth. The
citation about the church as the form of the glory of God was
interrupted at that point. Barth continues his thought by de-
scribing the form of the church as "proclamation, faith, confession, theology, prayer" *(loc. cit.)*. The "inner sphere" of the
church is marked off here as the location of glory (although the
sacraments certainly must also be considered here too). This is
quite correct. The *"testimonium spiritus sancti"* is first of all the
"testimonium internum": the life of faith, confession, theology,
and of prayer. Here the glory of God is primarily "at home"
in the church (for this also distinguishes it from any *"theatrum
magicum"* in that it does not shine or appear above our hearts

and heads but presses itself upon us, demanding personal response, personal appropriation and witness). *Doxa* accomplishes its goal in *doxazein*.

The fundamental form of this "glorification" is *proclamation*. Not only in the sense of preaching and the sacraments but of a "comprehensive evangelization." "Comprehensive" also means, as Reformed theology has always emphasized, that this proclamation is entrusted to all the people of God and may not be monopolized by any one group or class. One of the fathers of Reformed Orthodoxy, the (Czech) Basel theologian, Amandus Polanus (1561–1610), phrased it in a particularly fine way:

> God wishes that his glory be proclaimed: first of all by ministers of the Word of God. If the ministers are unwilling to do it, if the bishops are unwilling, the laymen will do it. If men are unwilling, women will do it. If the rich and mighty ones in this world are unwilling, the poor and needy ones will come forward. If the adults are unwilling, out of the mouths of babes and sucklings God will bring perfect praise for himself. If men and women will not do it, God will raise his sons out of the stones. He can establish the inanimate creatures themselves as the heralds of his glory. And indeed the heavens declare the glory of God. (*Syntagma theologiae christianae,* 1125)

2. An essential part of our response to the glory of God consists of its *diaconic* and *ethical* side. "Glorify God (also) in your body" (1 Cor. 6:20), says Paul in a concrete (sexual-ethical) context. And the Messiah, coming "in his glory," finds, according to Matthew 25:31–45, the response which accords with his glory only in those who have evidenced enough diaconic imagination and willingness to get involved. He finds this response in those who have actively come to the aid of the Son of Man in the "least of his brethren" and sisters.

"Ethics" and "diaconia" are to be understood comprehensively. Their classical form is certainly that of personally practiced neighborly love, turning to others in their individual distress, as admonished in Matthew 25. However, the more recent ecumenical emphasis upon the "structural aspects" of neighborly love and the social-ethical and political dimensions of diaconia is in my opinion also thoroughly legitimate. It also belongs to the foreground of the church's responsibility. This extension of the horizons corresponds to the "logic of glorification." It is not merely our individual situation which is illuminated by the "glory of God," but also the settings, relationships, and conditions in which we live, our whole "world of people." Not without reason, the "lordship of Christ" in the New Testament is emphatically related to the "powers and principalities": the glory of God shines into the realm of world history.

Let us take one concrete example for the exercise of this insight. It is not an accident that the great emphasis of Reformed theology (and before that of the Czech Reformation) upon the "honor of God" was more or less directly connected with "democratic consequences." The glory of God, embodied in the concrete history of Jesus Christ, encourages a "process of demythologization" in the political realm. If God alone should receive the honor, then every other claim to glory and lordship in either the church or society is subject to constant re-examination. Moreover, this can be taken in a positive sense. If the glory of God is the glory of the love of Christ, then we are obliged and encouraged to change and remove patiently and resolutely all loveless and graceless forms of domination between persons and groups of persons—first of all in the church but also in society.

3. To speak of an *"aesthetic dimension"* to the glorification of God sounds easily misunderstandable and quite suspicious to "Reformed ears." In order to reduce possible misunderstanding, I would like to emphasize at once that I am not espousing some kind of theological or romantic aestheticism. The glory of God is now a show which one could consume like a television

viewer. But we would lose an essential aspect if we were to overlook the fact that the most direct response to *doxa* is to be found in doxological behavior. And "doxology" means praise, adoration of the glory of God. A response which intends no predictable and exploitable purpose: the festival of freedom, the celebration of joy.

It is in such an attitude that the "aesthetic dimension" of glorification is contained. This can be clarified even further. In some of our catechisms, the following answer is given to the central (and the first!) question about the supreme end of human life: "Man's chief end is to glorify God, and to enjoy him forever" (Westminster Catechism). This is a notable formulation. The highest goal of our lives consists in *"Deum glorificare."* Yet in the very closest connection to that we find, *Deo frui*— an expression which looks back upon an ancient patristic tradition: "to enjoy God." An element of enjoyment, of pleasure, and of desire inheres in our response to the glory of God. God's pleasure in man is expressed in it (Luke 2:14), his "loving kindness" (Titus 3:4). It is only logical that, in the other direction, it arouses pleasure in God, the "friendliness towards God" of the believer.

Especially in our Reformed tradition we ought to emphasize more strongly this dimension of the glorification of God. Its unique value would compliment the other aspects of our tradition at an essential point. The glorification of God is comprised not only of missionary proclamation, not only of diaconic involvement, but also of praise and joy in what is beautiful. I agree with Jürgen Moltmann when he writes in regard to "The Lord of Glory":

> As the exalted, transfigured and transformed man of God, He saw His effect upon degraded, inhuman and mortal man not only through liberating power and new demands, but also through His perfection and His beauty. . . . These aesthetic categories of the resurrection belong to the new life of faith; without them, the discipleship of Christ and

the new obedience become joyless and legalistic labor (*Kirche in der Kraft des Geistes*, 128).

The Glory of God in Our World

The glory of God is acknowledged and confessed in the church. But this confession and this knowledge refer beyond the boundaries of the church. The church is the "basis" but not the "prison" of the glory of God. The light of *doxa* reaches further than to the four walls of the church. It "radiates through them," and makes them transparent. It has not only its ecclesiological but also *cosmological dimension.*

This direction is already present, as we saw in the Old Testament witness to the *kabod.* Whether indicatively, as in Isa. 6:3, or optatively, as in Psalm 72:19, the confession states that the glory of God is spread throughout the whole world. To prepare a way in the desert so that "the glory of the Lord shall be revealed and all flesh shall see it together"—that is, according to Deutero-Isaiah (40:3f.), the actual task of the prophet and his people.

In the New Testament, this Old Testament line is fully taken up. The light of the "glory of God in the face of Christ" is connected in Paul with the divine word of light of the Creator (2 Cor. 4:6). And in the eschatological perspective of *doxa,* it is not a temple which appears, but the city, and a new heaven and new earth: the new creation (Rev. 21). "God reaches His glorification in that the creation reaches its consummation" (J. Moltmann, *Evangelische Theologie,* 1975, 221).

With incomparable profundity this tension and connection between the church and the world, between man and nature, spirit and creation is testified to in Romans 8:19–30, a text whose ecumenical relevance is illustrated by the fact that it was chosen by the greatest number of participants at the Nairobi Assembly of the World Council of Churches as the basic theme for their Bible study. Both the community of fate and of hope within the creation is reflected upon here. The community of fate: "the whole creation," both the children of God and all of the rest of creation which suffers with them, "groan inwardly" (v. 23) under the enslaving power of sin and nothingness. But also the community of hope: all are drawn into the perspective of promise and participate in the renewing power of the Spirit "who helps us in our weakness" (v. 26). In this broad view of salvation, historical solidarity is dominated by the motif of the "glory of God." The "revealing of the sons of God" (v. 19) is the promise of liberation for all (v. 21). That means that the hope of glory is not meant merely for the church's "internal use"; it is not just churchly and not just human hope. It is the hope of all creation.

Perhaps we are theologically more open to these accents of the message of the glory of God today than we were a short time ago. Of course, they were clearly recognized by the Reformers, chiefly by Calvin; the statement about the world as the *theatrum gloriae Dei*" belongs to the classical Reformed heritage. But how often in later Protestantism, especially in Lutheranism, the cosmological dimension of the glory of God was ignored or even discounted as mythology which needed to be overcome existentially. In accordance with that, theology understood nature more often as the object of human domination than as the "stage of the glory of God" bound up with man at a far more profound level than that of the subject-object relationship. In such a way, nature was released, consciously or unconsciously, for technocratic exploitation.

The shock of the environmental crisis, which reveals the community of fate and hope of the whole creation drastically in view of the common dangers of destruction, forces us as judgment pronounced over us to think things through again and to repent. So we are beginning to take the dogmatic and ethical implications of Pauline thought more seriously again. The message of the glory of God is a motivation to think and act in responsibility for the future of the creation.

... And Our Future

This chapter was entitled "The Glory of God and Our Human Future." Let us conclude our argument by addressing ourselves to this particular concern in asking: What has the doxological prayer to say with respect to our uncertain future? I will do this by making three observations.

1. It is first necessary to make a *distinction*. When related to the question of human future, the biblical concept of the glory of God does not provide a patent pattern for futurological problems. What is at stake is the ultimate perspective, or to use a phrase of Karl Rahner, the "absolute future." We do not control this future, we cannot permanently fix it and certainly not manipulate it. We can only testify to it. In the glory of God man is promised the faithfulness, and the love of the triune God for his final distress, that of sin and of death.

It testifies to the fact that in Christ we will our future. Our fears and hopes of the future are not merely left in isolation or with anonymous powers of fate. We participate in Christ's death and resurrection. The creative power of the Spirit is present with us as a "warrant" (2 Cor. 1:22). Of course, "it does not yet appear what we shall be" (1 John 3:2). But we already know who is coming, and we know that we, when he comes, "will be like him." The future bears the characteristics of Jesus Christ.

The church lives with this message in view of the question of the future. In a well known ecumenical document this message was attested with the following words:

> Those who ask, "What will happen with the world?," we answer, "He, the King, stands before us." Those who ask, "What may we expect?," we answer, "We are not standing

before a pathless wilderness of unfulfilled time with a goal
which no one would dare to predict; we are gazing upon
our living Lord, our Judge and Savior, who was dead and
lives forevermore; upon the one who is come and is coming
and who will reign for ever. It may be that we shall encounter affliction; yes, that must be if we want to participate in Him. But we know His word, His royal word, "Be
comforted, I have overcome the world" (Christus, *Die
Hoffnung flur die Welt, Vorbereitungsdokument fur die 2.
Vollversammlung des Oekumeischen Rates der Kirchen,*
1954, I, A, 6).

2. This message is the heart of the Christian witness in
regard to the future of man: our essential, authentic, and irre-
placeable commission. But this commission would be seen too
narrowly and abstractly if it were oriented only to Christians.
It is also related to the concrete expectations of our other
contemporaries. Christians are not the only ones thinking about
the shape and structuring of the future of this world. And even
Christians do not think solely about the final eschatological
prospects of their lives. They also wonder about the historical
chances of the future for their children, their church, and their
society. They do not do this "in spite of their faith" (which
forbids only godless, self-centered care [Matt. 6:25f.]), but for
the sake of that faith. If the glory of God has appeared in the
history of Jesus of Nazareth, and if its history bears the characteristics of Jesus, then we are concerned with the "relative," the
earthly and day-by-day future of humanity. And therefore we
are not uninterested in the contemporary interpretations and
projects of the future.

Andre Dumas, in his study on our theme, referred to
various "models of the future" in contemporary thought: the
model of technocratic and social progress, asserting itself in
spite of failures; the model of an anti-industrial utopia which
reflects the negative effects of industrialization; and the model

or rather the horizon of a possible catastrophe. The very contemporary man signifies a widespread insecurity in view of the
future, which could be one of the typical hallmarks of the
second half of our century.

It is in this context, in the various concrete, cultural, and
social atmospheres of our countries, and thus in dialogue with
the various concrete models of the future, that we are to witness
to the message of the glory of God by participating in the cares
and the hopes of our contemporaries. *Nostra res agitur* wherever people are trying to break through the vicious circles that
are destroying their futures, and by looking ahead and planning
are trying to expand the future possibilities for themselves and
other creatures. If the glory of God does not provide pat an-
swers to questions of the future, it does encourage us to look
ahead, to plan, and to act in its perspective. With its reference
to the binding Word and the liberating history of Jesus it helps
to clarify priorities for this process of planning and acting.

3. Therefore *witness and involvement* define the structure
and content of Christian responsibility for the future. These two
motifs should be distinguished, but never separated from each
other. Witness to God's glory without involvement for the
future of humanity is empty. Involvement for the future without the perspective of the glory of God is blind. That which in
Jesus Christ God has bound together—his future with our
future—cannot be put asunder. Every kind of "uni-dimension-
ality" in our understanding of the future is limiting and impov-
erishing for both human existence and human hope. Let me
conclude by a word from John Calvin. In his *Institutes,* he
summarizes the existential relevance of our doxology for our
lives in the following words:

This is firm and tranquil repose for our faith. For if our
prayers were to be commended to God by our worth, who
would dare even mutter in his presence? Now, however

miserable we may be, though unworthiest of all, however devoid of all commendation, we will yet never lack a reason to pray, never be shorn of assurance, since his Kingdom, power and glory can never be snatched away from our Father (*Institutes* III, 20, 47).

It is good to live today and in the days of our uncertain future in the light and the power of this doxological certainty of our faith, in confessing: Thine is the Kingdom and the power and the glory *for ever and ever.*

The People Who Pray Are the People Who Hope

At the beginning of this book, I quoted the sentence of the old Karl Barth: "To clasp the hands in prayer is the beginning of an uprising against the disorder of this world." This is a remarkable sentence. It expresses the deep conviction that personal and social activities of Christians are deeply rooted in the spirit of prayer. At the same time, Barth's remark makes clear that the Christian life of prayer cannot remain a mere verbal operation. Prayer and endeavor, prayer and uprising, belong unseparably together. In both these directions, Christian life is characterized as the life in hope.

One old Latin saying states: *"Dum spiro spero"* (as long as I breathe, I hope). It is a moving expression of human courage refusing ever to give up. I admire this sentence. But I wonder whether it does not really say too much, overcharging human capacities. There are crushing situations in history, both individually and socially, in which human beings continue to breathe but give up any hope. Facing such situations, another sentence would be more realistic from a Christian point of view: *"Dum oro spero"* (as long as I pray, I hope). For prayer opens a dimension which cannot be closed by any predicament: it relates to, and invokes, the liberating presence of God transcending all human impasses. "For thine is the kingdom and

the power and the glory": Christian doxology, we recall, en-
larges human horizons and liberates us from the terminal
domination by historical kingdoms, powers, and glories—particularly those of sin and death. The prayer is the inner source
of hope, and vice versa.

This is the reason why we conclude our exposition of the
main motives of the Christian doxology by raising, in ecumenical context, the theme of hope.

The Crisis of Hope

The theme of hope is not a fashionable ecumenical topic
anymore. A decade ago, the situation seemed to be different. In
the sixties, the ecumenical preoccupation with hope seemed to
have the general backing of the spirit and mood of the times.
In all "the three worlds," there were hopeful signs of genuine
renewal in many churches and societies, new opportunities for
greater justice, freedom, and participation. The ecumenical
boat sailing towards Uppsala under the banner of "Behold, I
make all things new" took a lot of cultural wind into its sails.
In the seventies, however, the climate changed. Too many attempts at reform and renewal had been suppressed. Too many
hopes had been disappointed.

Today the question of the future presents itself in a whole
range of challenges which must be dealt with if there is to be
any future at all. I name only the most important ones: poverty
and hunger, by which the majority of our contemporaries are
deprived of even the most elementary possibilities of life; economic exploitation both in individual countries and on a world
scale; racist, political and ideological oppression, and the denial
of human rights in broad areas of our world; the threat to the
world itself as a consequence of our rapidly expanding capacity
for destruction and the devastation of our natural environment;
but also the creeping nihilism of meaningless lifestyles in the

midst of otherwise privileged, prosperous, and consumer-oriented societies.

There is another dimension to the crisis of hope today, a challenge not so much from the outside but from *within* the reflection on hope. There are some contemporaries who question not only particular hopes but *hope itself* as a legitimate human attitude.

Let me mention one recent example, a particularly moving one for me personally. Only a few months ago I received the posthumous papers of the Czech philosopher V. *Gardavsky.* Gardavsky was one of the Marxist participants in the Christian-Marxist dialogue in the sixties. He achieved fame with his book *God Is Not Yet Dead* in which he developed a very positive interpretation of biblical thought from Marxist standpoint. For him the figure of Jacob represented the creative model of humanity venturing to transcend all the historical, cultural, and religious boundaries in quest of richer human possibilities in quest of a model of dynamic hope. Written in the seventies, the posthumous papers confront us with an entirely different perspective. Gardavsky did not lose his interest in the Bible. But it is no longer Jacob who is the key figure but rather the prophet Jeremiah, "the man of sorrow," in captivity, an outsider both politically and religiously. For Gardavsky, Jeremiah is the antipode not only to Jacob but also to Prometheus, who is the mythological symbol at the roots of Western technocratic civilization in both its capitalist and Marxist versions. The disruptive consequences of that civilization have become increasingly obvious. We need to take a critical look at that Promethean heritage. It contains two constituent elements: the fire (= technology), but also the "blind hope." It is the combination of the two which leads to disaster, the *plus ultra* drive of insatiable technocrary. Therefore the conversion we need in order to be saved in our societies and on our planet is conversion from "blind hopes" and from hope altogether. Liberation from hope is the precondition of humane wisdom and survival. Gardavsky pleads for creative hopelessness, not in the sense of fashionable nostalgia or despair but in the sense of a patient and modest lifestyle stripped of assertive efforts and of illusions.

It is in this context of sharpened outward and inward challenge that we Christians are called to give an account of our hope today. It would be a meaningless undertaking if we were to disregard these challenges.

This undoubtedly increases the difficulty of our witness. When we try to speak of hope we run into cultural crosswinds. However, there is also another side to this. The same critical situation offers us a positive opportunity: the opportunity to become more concerned and more precise about the real ground of the hope within us. The days of facile hopes are frequently days when the churches are easily tempted to adapt their message of hope to the prevailing optimistic climate of their societies, to present *their* account of hope as one version of a general "principle of hope." The biblical "salt of hope" then loses much of its specific flavor, its true "saltness." I would see here a change offered to us in a changed situation: the radical challenge could lead us to seek a radical answer.

In the Christian understanding, "radical" means the "roots" of the church, the New Testament ground of hope. The cultural environment of the New Testament was not one of facile hopes. On the contrary, it was dominated by a fatalistic spirit. There were also profound questionings as to the legitimacy of human hope as such. Today's challenges to Christian hope are therefore nothing new in the history of the church. They could bring us nearer to a better understanding of the background and, still more important, to the common ground of the apostolic hope.

It is my task to introduce our discussions by drawing our attention to this common ground. The variety of concrete situations, which is so important as the context of specific expressions of our hope in each of our respective times and places, can hardly form the theme of an introductory statement. That will properly be the special concern of my fellow speakers from different regions. What I would like to present here are some essential aspects which, in my view, should not be omitted in any of our accounts, however necessary it is to emphasize different things in different situations. As point of departure and focus, I wish to refer to one central text expressive of the New Testament hope: 1 Timothy 4:10: "That is why we struggle and work hard, because we have set our hope on the living God, who is the Saviour of all men, especially of those who believe."

Three points seem to me to be of particular importance: 1. The ground of hope; 2. Dimensions of hope; 3. Hope and freedom, in action and in suffering.

The Ground of Hope

In the apostolic perspective there is no ambiguity whatever about the *ground of hope:* "We have set our hope on the living God." In clear contrast to its secular use, the New Testament word *elpis* does not mean a changeable "floating" attitude with an uncertain background. Christian hope is rooted neither in potentialities of nature nor in the creativity of human history. It is not matter which is "the mother of hope" (E. Bloch). Still less is it the sum total of human achievements or the quality of the religious consciousness. There are human expectations which can be built on such foundations and they have their due importance for human life. But hope in the biblical sense has a quite specific anchorage. *Hope and God are inseparable:* to be "without God in the world" means to be without hope (Eph. 2:12). The symbolism of the anchor as the sign of Christian hope rests concretely on one basis: "We have set our hope on the living God."

When Korean Presbyterian Christians invited theologians

of the World Alliance of Reformed Churches to attend the 1979 Theological Consultation on the theme of Hope, they formulated the topics in a particularly poignant way: "The Hope: God's Suffering in Human Struggles." This is a remarkable formulation. Not only is the unseparable connection between God and hope expressed unambiguously. Our hope is rooted in God's involvement in human struggles. The formulation goes still further and elucidates the crucial and liberating way of God's involvement: his participation in suffering. In this motif we doubtlessly encounter the heartbeat of the biblical faith in God in its difference to general religion. Already in the Old Testament the God of Israel was testified as the One who goes with and suffers with his people. And in the New Testament this understanding reaches its peak in the passion of Jesus Christ and in his death on the cross. Hence the cross is literally the Cruz or better: the *proprium christianum* of the Christian concept of God. The "living God" of the Apostolic message is the "compassionate" God. If a concept of God is not capable of expressing this "com-passion" of God, it is disqualified as a Christian concept of God.

On this central point there was a parting of ways—already in the early church and actually throughout the whole history of Christian doctrine. The early Church Fathers were faced with an immensely difficult task in their philosophical environment. For the existing concepts—those of the Graeco-Roman antiquity—in no way fulfilled the necessary requirements. On the contrary, in their sublime philosophical-metaphysical emphasis they uncompromisingly excluded any compassion and any capability of suffering by God. God cannot suffer. His metaphysical state is not compatible with suffering—and even less with compassion. *Apatheia* is the basic attitude of the metaphysical God. The classical doctrine of God is developed under the premises of the "axiom of apathy."

The weight of this philosophical heritage also burdened

the Christian history of dogma. It was extremely difficult to fight against this heritage. The trinitarian concept of God played an important role in this spiritual struggle. In the trinity the passion of Jesus Christ—the fate of the Son—is taken up in a central way. The implication of this, however, is that God is not a being divorced from suffering, not an apathetic being. God's being is in suffering. In this sense a true "revolution in the concept of God" occurs in trinitarian thinking.

This revolution was very early and very often picked up and neutralized, as so many authentically biblical ideas and motifs. Today we have every reason to take up these impluses again and continue them. The theologians of the Third World, particularly from Asia, have made (and have still to make) a substantial ecumenical contribution (see Kazoh Kitamuri's *Theology of the Pain of God.* John Knox Press, 1965) in this respect.

This task is not only valid in view of the authentic biblical origin of theology. It is also true in view of the special need of our witness in modern society. I am thinking of the necessary encounter with *atheism.* One of its especially poignant and justified themes is the protest against God in the name of the suffering creation. This theme is raised passionately (or silently), for instance, by Dostoyevsky or Camus, but also by innumerable of our contemporaries. I consider this protest to be basically justified and appropriate. Theology and the church have every reason to listen to this understandingly. Such a listening is not possible, except in a self-critical way. Indeed has not Christian theology actually provoked this protest by advocating—against its better judgment—an apathetic concept of God? The passionate protest in the name of the suffering creation is entirely applicable to an apathetic God. On this point evangelical Protestants can hardly do otherwise than align themselves with the atheistic protestors! "Without Jesus I would be an atheist" (J. Gottschick).

But Jesus, and the belief in God which we gain from the story of his life and death, is quite different. In him we encounter the God to whom no human suffering is foreign. To be confronted by this God in view of the suffering of creation— and in one's own suffering—does not mean to be thrown into the deadly void of absolute apathy, but rather to experience the abundance of divine sympathy. The justified protest of the atheists does not really reach the living God. On the contrary, this God anticipated this protest against the powers of death in the Easter events by exposing himself to the attacks of death. Thus he restored the right of the suffering creation and placed its destiny in the eschatological perspective of the hope of resurrection and liberation (Romans 8:18f.).

We have every reason not to hide this eschatological light under a bushel. It contains liberating power and potential, an element of the "nevertheless" even in apparently hopeless situations. To say "Yes!" to God in faith and hope means to say "No!" to death and its allies, the "principalities and powers" of sinful destruction and oppression. It is an invitation to act accordingly. In Christ's liberating name there is the ultimate "tomorrow" which no natural or supernatural power can finally forbid. The very naming of the living God, therefore, strengthens "the murmur revealing that the victory of the night is not complete." It lays the foundations and broadens the horizon of the human future, counteracts the spirit of fatalism and nihilism.

The Dimensions of Hope

The second issue I should like to discuss briefly is the question of the *dimensions of hope, the range of hope.* The apostolic affirmation I am referring to is the continuation of the previous words: *"Who is the Savior of all men, especially of those who believe?"* At first glance, this looks like an example of awkward logic. It speaks first "of *all*" but then, as if afraid of its own boldness, it speaks "especially of *some.*" Clearly it works with two accents, distinguishes two dimensions of the horizon of hope. But, precisely in this "irresolute," "open-ended" way, it is faithful to the dynamics characteristic of the New Testament treatment of the relation between church and world. In our accounting for hope, both aspects of this statement should be respected.

I start with the little word "especially." The biblical vision of hope is related "especially to those *who believe.*" When we were considering the "ground of hope" we already stressed that hope is not an abstract human virtue, a general predicate of the human psyche or of history. Hope and the living God—the Savior—belong together. The "movement of hope" initiated in the name of the living God is not a chaotic *Sturm and Drang* ("storm and stress") but a structured and disciplined mission. It is rooted in the apostolic faith; it is carried out in the apostolic way. It has to be accounted for. Hope, therefore, can neither be limited to a private inward matter of the isolated individual nor dissolved in cosmopolitan generalities. It initiates the "third way," that of a "committed fellowship," of Christian brotherhood and sisterhood. God's vision and mission of hope calls forth a concrete human agency, the "people of God," the "people of hope": the church, for the God of hope is the Savior *especially* of those who believe.

But it would be a misunderstanding of this apostolic "especially" if we were to isolate it from the preceding words "who is the Savior *of all men.*" The legitimate "specialness" of the church does not mean an exclusive privilege or even monopoly of hope. Established Christendom has throughout its history tended to draw such a conclusion; its representatives have presented themselves as the proprietors of hope and the managers of salvation. Such an attitude distorts the biblical concepts of both hope and salvation. In the New Testament there is no monopoly of hope. We find there the dynamics of the Spirit, and, above all, the dynamics of hope—inspiring believers to witness to hope and to serve hope. The "especially" applied to Christians confers no privilege of ownership but only the privilege of mission. This mission points beyond the boundaries of the church. The light of the eschatological hope reaches much further than the four walls of the church. It "radiates through them" and makes them transparent. The hope of Israel becomes the hope of all nations. In the ultimate perspective of the New Testament hope, what appears is not a temple but the city of God and a new heaven and a new earth: the new creation (Rev. 21). The God of the believers is the God for all.

This dynamic tension between the apostolic "all" and the apostolic "especially" is also very important for our accounting for hope today. It reminds us that we confess a hope which is entrusted in a special sense to the church, the hope of the church and for the church. Our accounting for hope would cut loose from its mornings and lose its credibility if it were to "float" in cosmopolitan (or vaguely ecumenical) clouds without manifest connections with the life of our actual churches. We are all aware that this is not at all easy. A glance at most of our churches, especially those in traditional and affluent countries, is far from encouraging. And yet: *Hic Rhodus, hic salta!* This is where the witness of hope begins: at the grass roots of hope, in our churches. Their present conditions can be painful for us; we can struggle with them and about them; but we cannot give them up. To do so would be to lose the home base of hope. The presence of congregations of the people of God within a society and their witness to the name of the living God in that society makes a difference to its spiritual and cultural climate.

At the same time, the apostolic "Savior of all" reminds us of the radically open horizon of hope. The church is the cradle but not the tomb of hope: its base but not its prison. A merely ecclesial account of hope would miss the dynamics of its theme. Here the ecumenical dimension and movement of hope becomes important in its search both for the unity of the church and for the unity of humankind. An account of hope which lacks a conscious relationship to a concrete "local" communion easily becomes empty; an account of hope without an ecumenical horizon easily becomes "blind." The apostolic message can help us to face up to both these dangers: "Who is the Savior of all men, especially of those who believe?"

Hope and Freedom: In Action and Suffering

There is a third constitutive element in the apostolic account of hope: the witness to the ground of hope and the statement about the range of hope lead the apostle *"to struggle and to work hard."* This is strong language: the Greek words refer to drudgery and to a life-and-death struggle, to human action and to human suffering. The setting for the apostolic witness of hope is not conditions of good fortune and easy comfort. Hope opens up the narrow way of Christian freedom in action and suffering too, especially in adverse situations.

Hope opens up the narrow way of freedom. It struck me how often in the recent ecumenical discussions the motif of hope is connected with the motif of freedom. I think of the Faith and Order Conference in Bangalore, 1978 in which I was very active (its deliberations are very much in the background of this book). It is no accident that the ecumenical "theology of hope" paved the way for the ecumenical "theology of liberation" (and *vice versa*). There is a biblical reason for this: for the witnesses of the New Testament there is an intimate connection between the hope set on the living God and the practice of freedom. "That is why we struggle and work hard." Biblical salvation implies hope of freedom and freedom of hope.

When hope and freedom are so closely related, what does this mean for our understanding of both these terms? Two accents of the key words "hope of freedom" must be distinguished and connected. First, in the biblical understanding of hope there is always an element of the *"not yet."* The life of a Christian in hope and freedom is no automatic progress and triumphal procession. It is a "narrow way" which is constantly menaced from within and without; hope in the struggle, freedom under the cross. It is striking that the central promises of salvation and liberation in the New Testament at the same time soberly declare the depth of the human predicament: "We know that the whole creation groans with the pain like the pain of childbirth until now" (Rom. 8:22). And in Romans 7, with reference to the Apostle's own life: "I see in my body another law . . . making me captive to the law of sin" (7:23). No doubt: the human world is, objectively and subjectively, a deeply estranged world. The idealists and the optimists are therefore mistaken when they argue: I ought, therefore I can. The real human condition is different: "I don't do the good I want to do; instead, I do the evil I do not want to do. . . . Wretched man that I am!" (Rom. 7:19, 24). There is no euphoria of freedom in the New Testament. Freedom takes place in hope.

And yet: although the biblical vision of the human situation bars the way to idealism and optimism, in doing so it does not in any way direct us to enter the opposite camp of the pessimists and the "realistics." I think of those programs and attitudes which, seeing the conditions of human bondage and the risks of freedom, fatalistically freeze them, recommending authoritarian reactions and structures. If you enter the human world, take the whip or the bomb with you. Such a "realistic" philosophy and practice is incompatible with the Christian vision of hope. There is the other element in the Christian hope of freedom. There is not only the "not yet," there is also the *"already"* of the promise and the commitment of the living God. The apostolic message is clear about it—precisely in the passage which we quoted as reflecting the depth of the human predicament. The bondage of the creation is radical and universal—and yet, it is by no means "stabilized" but rather oriented "towards hope" (Rom. 8:20).

The sigh of Paul—"Wretched man that I am!"—is deep; and yet, it is not his last word; it is followed immediately by: "Thanks be to God through Jesus Christ our Lord!" (Rom. 7:25). Humanity is not a *massa preditionis,* damned for all eternity, but it exists rather in all its predicament already "in hope," under the impact of God's salvation, under the promise of an "unforbiddable tomorrow." There is a *hope* for freedom.

I am convinced that both the accents of hope just mentioned should shape our account of hope. The first aspect is already worth considering with its sobering "eschatological reservation." Under the conditions of history, the hope of liberation must always be seen as an open engagement but never as a perfected "realm of freedom." In church history, particularly in the secularized movements of Western Christianity, the lack of sober clarity on this score has been considerable. Engagement for progress and freedom, and the relative achievements of progress and freedom have been hailed as the emerging secular salvation, and precisely because of this have been corrupted. How often has a movement of freedom turned into an established repression? In many a freedom fighter of the past and present there appears a future oppressor of freedom. Ernst Bloch expressed this experience in 1930 with the following words: "In the *citoyen* there was a hidden *bourgeois.*" Heaven forbid what perhaps is hidden in the pious Christian crusader!). This experience is not to be misused in a defeatist and even cynical way to point to the futility of all historical involvement. However, we must remain sober and free in it, without absolutizing our cause and our achievements.

Even more important, perhaps, is the other, *positive accent* of hope. Unless I am very much mistaken, the real threat to freedom in our world comes not so much from the idealists of freedom but rather from the political fatalists and cynical despisers of freedom. True enough, they hold many trump cards in their hands; the prospects of freedom in the contemporary world are not all that bright. At the beginning I mentioned a whole series of discouraging features. It is no wonder that growing tendencies towards fatalistic power-politics, with the corresponding feelings of the powerlessness and futility of all commitment, are growing and even prevailing in many places.

In such a setting, a Christian account of hope can prove as important and as relevant today as it did in the not so very dissimilar conditions and atmosphere of apostolic times. The apostolic hope was then and is now a resistance movement against fatalism. In the perspective of the living God and his liberating involvement in the Christ event, fate is broken. The "principalities and powers" (Rom. 8:38) no longer possess the ultimate key to human or cosmic possibilities. They are powerful; sinful elements and oppressive structures in history must be taken seriously. But they are not omnipotent. They cannot "separate us from the love of God" (Rom. 8:39). We are not left alone in our struggles. God suffers and acts with us. There is hope for freedom and freedom for hope. That is why we do not need to be resigned, in spite of everything. That is why we struggle and work hard—in the hope set firmly on the living God: For thine is the Kingdom and the Power and the Glory.